9 Tips
for Entrepreneurs to Improve Work Efficiency:

Work Smarter, Not Harder

Joe Chan

From the voice of a REAL Small Business Owner

© Copyright Joe Chan - AES Publishing 2020 - All rights reserved.

The content contained within this book may not be reproduced, duplicated or transmitted without direct written permission from the author or the publisher.

Under no circumstances will any blame or legal responsibility be held against the publisher, or author, for any damages, reparation, or monetary loss due to the information contained within this book. Either directly or indirectly. You are responsible for your own choices, actions, and results.

Legal Notice:

This book is copyright protected. This book is only for personal use. You cannot amend, distribute, sell, use, quote or paraphrase any part, or the content within this book, without the consent of the author or publisher.

Disclaimer Notice:

Please note the information contained within this document is for educational and entertainment purposes only. All effort has been executed to present accurate, up to date, and reliable, complete information. No warranties of any kind are declared or implied. Readers acknowledge that the author is not engaging in the rendering of legal, financial, medical or professional advice. The content within this book has been derived from various sources. Please consult a licensed professional before attempting any techniques outlined in this book.

By reading this document, the reader agrees that under no circumstances is the author responsible for any losses, direct or indirect, which are incurred as a result of the use of the information contained within this document, including, but not limited to, — errors, omissions, or inaccuracies.

Just For You

Hi, I'm Joe Chan and thanks for grabbing a copy of my "Work Smarter, Not Harder" self-help book. If you planning to exhibit in a tradeshow, this will be perfect guide for you, "The Ultimate Exhibitor Guide: Tradeshow Planning Checklist and Worksheet"! It's absolutely FREE! Before we get to it, I'd like to give a quick introduction about myself – who I am and what you can expect from this guide.

In a nutshell, I have been in the tradeshow industry for over 15 years. My company's name is called Artsoft Expo Solutions Inc. (www.artsoft.ca). We provide complete tradeshow display solutions – from off-the-shelf portable display to fully customized structure system. You can visit our Facebook page at www.facebook.com/artsoftexpo for some of the displays we have built in the last 15 years. Due to the pandemic, my business has been at a halt. However, it actually gives me time to sit down and rethink what I would like to do in my next 15 years. I came across an idea of self-publishing and I would love to share my personal tradeshow experience and hopefully will inspire some of you.

Everything I said in this guide came from my own personal experience of planning a tradeshow or exhibition. With this planning checklist and worksheet, I hope I can help save you some invaluable time and that you can acquire more ROI from your next tradeshow.

Let's get into the Ultimate Tradeshow Planning Checklist and Worksheet now! I hope you enjoy this guide.

SIGN UP NOW @ http://www.artsoft.ca/exhibitinglife/

Contents

Just For You	6
INTRODUCTION	11
Chapter 1 Be Honest To Yourself (And Customers)	17
Chapter 2 Perfect Is Imperfect	27
Chapter 3 Planning with Time	41
Chapter 4 Build A Mind That Sequence Multitask	53
Chapter 5 Time Management with different skills and tools	65
Chapter 6 Manage Distraction - Not to AVOID it	75
Chapter 7 Learn To Say 'Yes' When It Is A 'No'	87
Chapter 8 Taking A Break	97
Chapter 9 Organizing Your Work With No-Cost Online Organizational Tool	109
CONCLUSION	126
References	134

INTRODUCTION

Alvin just got home after a long and stressful day at work; he looked up at the clock and felt that he just didn't get enough done. He has been working overtime and still not hitting the target outcome.

As he walked from the sitting room to the bedroom, Alvin continued thinking, "why haven't I discovered how to improve efficiency at work? What has made this difficult? What am I doing wrong?"

Alvin was one of many business owners who finds it hard to develop an effective and more streamlined way of managing their work-related tasks. If you are also having a hard time with this, you may think there is seemingly no end in sight. But it tends to be if you follow the footsteps of individuals who have prevailed over it.

It seems like more companies are adopting the motto "do more with less." So, where does that leave you?

In today's fast-paced work environment, it seems like we can never find enough hours in the day to complete the tasks we are assigned. Long to-do lists and constant meetings can make it extremely difficult to finish all our work on time. While it's difficult, there are ways to be more efficient at work and leave at 5 pm instead of spending hours working overtime.

As daylight savings approaches and 2021 is well halfway through, it's a good time to think about different ways to, well, save time. These days, entrepreneurs are spending more time in the office, certainly going beyond the usual 40 hours per week. However, the increase in hours worked does not necessarily translate into greater efficiency.

There is nothing more important to a small business than its employees. If your employees are happy, your productivity will increase, and that's exactly what you need to help your business grow.

Making small changes to your habits will significantly improve office efficiency and productivity in your business. These changes will let you get more quality work done in a shorter amount of time and reduce the time spent on unnecessary tasks.

I specifically wrote this book to help those who are:

- Business owners who feel you are working longer hours but not have an equal amount of productivity output.

- Entrepreneurs looking for inspiration to help identify inefficiency and provide a possible methodology to find solutions that fit.

- Looking for new ideas and solutions

- Looking for real, small business examples from an actual small business owner

This book is a self-improvement plan to help you to work more efficiently with more productivity output.

Ultimately, the purpose is to inspire you with the methodology. Below are examples of what you will gain from reading this book:

- You will gain knowledge from someone's experience and re-use that knowledge to apply to your own business challenge.

- You will learn to work more efficiently, get more things done and generate more profit while reducing expenses.

- You will discover a system to help rethink what you have been doing. A systematic way to do a re-evaluation/re-assessment.

I have been running my business for more than 20 years, starting when I was 19. I started with building computers and selling computer parts, then went into website development and expanded into becoming a print broker. Now, I'm in tradeshow display manufacturing and large format printing.

I hope to share my experience and examples to inspire you to think differently. I also hope you can use some of my ideas and workflow to improve efficiency in your business.

Almost all business professionals claim to have "productivity hacks" that can assist you in getting more done in less time. No doubt, there are some common-sense tools you can implement to be more productive. Things like taking short breaks, creating effective to-do lists, and resisting social media.

I've discovered some main strategies you can implement to become more productive. Still, it's essential not to consider these tips as "hacks." There is no trick to becoming more productive. There are only new habits we can implement to try to be better, more efficient employees. By developing some of these habits, you are taking the proper steps to become more productive.

So, how can leaders and managers enhance productivity while still saving time? It all starts with a detailed plan and a willingness to commit to that plan. Here are nine chapters to help you move in the appropriate direction. To help you improve work efficiency, work smarter and not harder. I hope this book is helpful to you.

Chapter 1
Be Honest To Yourself (And Customers)

"Being honest with yourself may not get you many customers, but it will always get you the right ones."

Often, we want a business to skyrocket. We want to impress. We want to keep our customers' loyalty, so we tell them, and ourselves, what we want to hear. However, over time, even as we lie and deceive ourselves, we find that things don't go the way we plan

You don't necessarily need to see the whole staircase, just take the first step. - Martin Luther King Jr. People don't get fat overnight and cannot by some magical power lose weight. It takes time, and they know it, so what do they do? They take one step at a time, one squat, one push-up to get their desired body weight, physical fitness level or shape. Your priority as an entrepreneur is to start and build up gradually, but no, we want to go once and go big. However, this is the biggest lie we tell ourselves. It's ok that we have big goals, but the steps should be small and steady. Try not to create big plans back-to-back every day. Doing this will actually diminish your work efficiency.

We often adore the word, ' busy. ' So we try to fill our days unnecessarily with as many trivial pursuits as we can. Yeah, you're very busy—another sincere lie. When our co-employees, friends or employees ask us what we will be doing for the weekend, we come up with a list containing many activities. We try as much as we can to complete these very insignificant duties that sometimes leave us tremendously tired, mentally and physically. In the end, we barely have enough time to carry out essential tasks when they arrive. We feel that the only way to be productive is to have our days overbooked. It's even worse when we set out to achieve an impossible task at the end of the day because, let's be honest, we never get to perform them anyway, and the end result is a whole lot of frustration. As a business owner, time spent away from work is not a loss, like you think it might be, but offers many benefits. You relax, recharge and replenish to produce a better result and increase your work efficiency.

You think to yourself, the more, the merrier. You know, and can feel it in the depth of your heart, that you have many jobs at hand. What do you do? You accept more jobs. And why do you do that? Because you want to secure your customers because more customers mean more money. You normalize the intense pressure you feel as you are hardworking. At the end of the day, you deliver mediocre or incomplete work, sometimes not delivering at all. You are aware, and you have a job at hand. Focus solely on making it the best you can. The idea is on quality, not quantity. You want to leave the customer satisfied, happy and willing to recommend you to someone else to assure your work efficiency and quality. Don't accept more and accomplish less.

Tomorrow is another day. Yeah, right. Now, face the mirror and tell yourself that is a white lie. 'Tomorrow might be too late' is the slogan. We almost always procrastinate, projects, launchings, major tasks and even minor ones. We can get these tasks done as soon as possible. Still, we leave them because we believe we can do it later, in a few hours, in a few days, in a few weeks; how about one month or one more year? And you know what happens, we get very little to nothing done. You tell yourself, the project was too large to finish in one year. Meanwhile, you could have done it perfectly in 6 months, but you kept procrastinating.

In reality, procrastination might be our only obstacle. As entrepreneurs, we are rarely accountable to anyone but ourselves. It's our business, after all. We could finish this task or launch this project tomorrow instead, just after getting this little task done. I mean, it's just one more day, right? Tomorrow will be a good day. You are relaxed and taking your time because no one but you know how little or slow your progress is (if you have even begun at all). This 'last minute' attitude eventually becomes your habit. You hold a client or dodge them because you haven't completed or have not even started a job. Before you are fully aware of the effect of your behaviour, you have lost a lot of clients as you have lost your credibility with them. Be honest to yourself. If you cannot complete a job without some pressure, watch or mentorship, get one! Let your business partner or associate know. They can exert some pressure on you. You can also get a friend to ensure you get your jobs completed on time. Aside from that, you can break down your goals into doable mini-tasks on a to-do list and, most importantly, set deadlines. You know you have a specific deadline to meet. You work tirelessly towards achieving that goal. The feeling of having finished successfully is like a burden lifting from your shoulders.

When other people lie to us, we want to smash their heads, and we look at them with so much hate in our eyes because obviously, they have betrayed us. However, we lie to ourselves, and it's the most pleasant thing we have ever heard. We give excuses for our shortcomings and continually console ourselves that we were too tired, that we didn't have the resources, that we're not perfect and worse of all, that we are humans. Our ever-ready response, 'I'm a human being, and all human beings make mistakes.' Doing that, we are like children that never own up to our mistakes. To improve your work efficiency, you have to recognize and accept that it's lower than expected and that you indeed need improvement. When we make mistakes, we should look at them with a critical eye, find out where we erred, and correct our errors with conscious effort and energy. We are apt to leaning towards a perfect idea of ourselves in front of others. We want to be the business owner who knows what he or she is doing. We aim to be the entrepreneur who knows the market like the back of their hand or the employer who thoroughly understands the workings of their organization or the minds of their employees. When we fail woefully, we look for who to shift the blame to, often resulting in the client to vent or blame. Let your clients see you accept your mistakes and make corrections. That way, they know you value getting better over getting cash.

Many ways are available to get to the market, and I mean this literally. Don't be so stuck on the idea that everyone is doing it this way, especially when you know it's not working for you. Holding steadfastly to business stereotypes will get you nowhere. The uniqueness of every business lies in its creativity and singularity. Don't deceive yourself, standing rigid to ideas that you know are not favourable to you because everyone else does them. Be realistic. A coin has two sides, and the coin is collected by the seller back or front. Believing your time will come without trying out other ideas is simply being judgmental to other ideas when you haven't even tried them.

The worst lie we tell ourselves, though, is to do something because someone else has done it, even when we know that we don't enjoy doing it. Most entrepreneurs and business owners jump into jobs because they've heard how it got someone millions, or a house, or a car. We don't genuinely love the job, so we are not genuinely interested in what we're doing. We work all day and get home irritated or frustrated because we derive absolutely no joy from what we do. Before you get into a business, you must tell yourself that it's best you find something your heart will be interested in.

Don't lie to your customers. A product is not good, let your customers know. A product is not available, let your customers know. If something is not the way it should be, let your customers know. Often, in a bid to keep our customers coming back, we lie to them. They usually don't realize they are being deceived, and you enjoy the fruits of your deceits. However, when they find out, I can most assuredly say, you have lost a customer for life. Being utterly sincere with them is the key to winning their trust and respect. They might not necessarily buy from you then, but they are aware that whatever happens, you would always be sincere, and this keeps them coming back. Sometimes, the quality of our products is compromised, maybe due to an unexpected mistake or delay. Relaying to our customers or clients, the supposed reduction or the reason for a postponement earns us more respect. They treat you not just as a mere seller now but as a friend. However, if you feel like this is difficult to achieve, when a product is not good enough or up to standard, don't give it out. Tell them bluntly that it's not available. Your client values your advice, quality and relationship. Don't lose that. The better your rapport is with your client, the better your productivity and work efficiency.

Don't let your customers lie to you. If a client is trying to take you for granted, it's best to let them know that you are not comfortable with them. We often forget that more customers can come at any time. So let go of customers who may manipulate us into prices or business deals that aren't favourable. Sometimes, we try to be smarter than these customers and twist words and business deals, but eventually, they will find out and be mad. You haven't only lost that one customer but other customers as well. He or she is in the market and can talk to prospective clients before you know it about your deceit, tactfully excluding their part in the whole charade. Now your business productivity and work efficiency are affected. Set boundaries with your customers. Let them know your worth and stand your ground. Nothing is worth sacrificing your reputation for because, in the long run, it's not just the product but your business reputation and brand name that sells.

'The risk is high. I don't have professional skills. I will have no time for myself'. **These are just some of the petty lies prospective business owners tell themselves.** Be honest; if you never start, you will never get to know. The risk with starting up a business is the same as the risk associated with working in a company under a salary. The truth is, if you don't put in more effort with a salary job as you do with your own business, you will be fired. Entrepreneurship is not as tedious as other people make it to be. You work as hard as you do with a salary job. The only difference is a more flexible schedule, and you don't need professional skills. You just need the determination to be the best and most influential worker. And there you are, good to go!

Here are a few tips I will leave with you before we move on;

Never lie to your customer - 9 out of 10 times, you think you will get away with it. Nope! You will get caught. The nine times you didn't get caught, either your customer didn't tell you about it and never came back, or the customer never returned and gave you a poor review to friends and family.

You might think being sincere with customers is not work efficiency-related. Still, you need to put double the effort not to get caught every time you try to hide something. Possibly one lie after the other. Yes, it will work if you only have 10 or even 100 customers. What happens if you're dealing with 500 or 1000 customers?

Here is an example of what I mean. Say you're trying to make an extra buck from this particular customer because you know they have a higher budget, or they can spend more money. You already set a standard price list, but you want to make more money from this customer, so you add in some hidden extra charges. Now guess what, they come back to you and ask you about it. You have to spend double your time to figure out how to answer or cover your lies. So that's not efficient. Of course, it's also not ethical. But people have their own reasons to support this action. We are not discussing this from a moral perspective, purely from an efficiency perspective. Don't be greedy. Follow your set goal and be a long-term thinker.

Chapter 2
Perfect Is Imperfect

"Have no fear of perfection - you'll never reach it."

It's reasonable and often necessary to work towards perfection and strive to get a particular outstanding goal. However, we scrutinize our work through a magnifying glass. Continually edit and rewrite, re-strategize and re-plan. We wait for the perfect time to launch our business, refuse other people's ideas because obviously, they aren't to our taste. We go on a never-ending fault-finding journey on our employees' or teammates' plans or work. However, nothing is perfect if we are completely honest with ourselves. Like Salvador Dali said, ' Have no fear of perfection - you'll never reach it.'

Waiting for the perfect moment, perfect website, perfect design, perfect customers, or consumers is just deadly. Our companies or products, in that case, may never see the light of day. In simple terms, while waiting for the right time, we may never actually get them out there. Working so hard to get the perfect conditions, we lose sight of the main goal: getting your business or product out there, in the market where your customers or consumers are.

Having a quality product is key. Having a perfect product, now that is impossible. If Jeff Bezos, the founder of Amazon, were bent on getting the perfect products to the perfect consumers, he would have never started. Sometimes, even when we order right now, we might not get exactly what we ordered. I'm sure you know the famous Amazon 'WTF moments' when what you ordered isn't what you got. We still unrelentingly order from Amazon. We do this is because the company name is familiar to us, and we overlook the glitches. We are pretty attached to Amazon in some way, having used it before other similar business ideas popped up. Now, suppose

Jeff Bezos had decided to wait to get the perfect conditions. In that case, he releases the business today. He begins to hassle to establish a brand name amongst other already similar thriving businesses in the marketplace, or worse, he never launches Amazon. You don't want to exhaust precious time and resources trying to be perfect. It slows you down. The idea of getting a perfect product keeps you in that one spot, constantly being hypercritical. There might be someone who has the same idea or is building on a similar idea. Your only advantage might be you pushing it out into the market and winning the consumer's choice awards before your competitor gets his/her plans together.

Variety is the spice of life. Most people tend to love a dynamic and relatable business, product, advert or business owner than a perfect one. Why? It's simple, their spontaneity. They never know what new ideas will pop up, and boy, are they looking forward to it. Humans love change. They are constantly looking for something new to commend or criticize. They relate the most with the brand they see. Taking your sweet time to obsess over every minute brings you no closer to them. Your customers are essential to your growth and production process. Put your business out there and let them hit hard, praise and backlash. The important thing is that you take action and let them see it. Otherwise, how will you ever get feedback? How will you improve your work efficiency? Your customers will let you know what changes need to be made, albeit, the biting criticism and tough love.

I would like to think that you understand deeply that an entrepreneur has to take risks. Sometimes, your reason for the impossible standard you have set is the fear of failure and criticism. 'What if Mrs. A says it's not good enough?', 'What if the business crashes?', you ask yourself. News flash: if Mrs. A criticizes your product and she makes a valid point, work on it and make it better. That is the purpose of criticism. If it crashes, you can now pick the pieces up, go back to the drawing board and pay attention to your mistakes. But you need to take action, move your butt and stop being stagnant trying to make it better, or you just never know.

When you work with a team or a set of people, you and your employees must have a healthy mindset. When you beat the crap out of your mind by nitpicking and twitching over minor details, you tend to wear yourself and your teammates out with your perfectionistic tendencies. In all that mental exhaustion, there is likely little or no room for creativity, pooling of ideas, innovation and most importantly, change and improvement. You embark on a notorious fault-finding journey with every idea any of them brings up. In your head, this has to be the perfect method. You begin to invest your limited time, energy, and resources into making sure that you have the perfect, outstanding idea, strategy, or plan. You and your teammates work furiously and tirelessly towards your 'big idea' with no room for thinking from another perspective. You end up debilitated. Your team ends up exhausted and out of energy. When trying to find the perfect idea, you lose time, energy, and resources.

When you work so hard towards perfection, in business or production, and you finally put it out there, chances are your expectations high. You expect perfect results. You expect the outcome to be mind-blowing. If it's not or doesn't come out the way you wish, the disappointment and pain you feel are staggering. Your mental and physical health is strongly threatened. Your confidence is considerably bruised because you had unrealistic, sky-scraping goals. You have to understand that your business and products, especially when entering the labour market, are like babies. When you put them to stand, they may stand (go as planned, achieved goals), walk (go beyond your imagination) or fall (go below your expectations). Like parents to these businesses, you feel sad and frustrated for a little while when they fall. Still, you pick them up and continue to nurture and build them to that level where they stand or, surprisingly, walk. You certainly don't expect them to run, swim or fly but waiting for the conditions to be perfect prevents their movement and, subsequently, their growth.

In your bid to release the absolute best to your consumers/customers, you decide to take your time. You are waiting for your product to look its best. You are waiting for the 'right' time and opportunity. You see another product with better features than the ones you have set in place. You decide to wait and improve on your product, adding that feature. You keep doing this until you eventually feel you can never get it right and that your mind, products and ideas are mediocre. You may even become totally unwilling to launch your business or products, feeling they will never be up to the proper standard or taste. This feeling diminishes your self-confidence and esteem. The startling truth is, you can't predict, with a hundred percent accuracy, the market's reaction to your product. Human taste varies from time to time. When you feel your product will never be up to standard, the likelihood of creating another is very slim. It diminishes your passion and dampens your creativity.

Perfection simply kills passion. The lack of creativity is because you don't love what you do anymore. The constant struggle of backbreaking scrutiny of your business idea or product sucks and drains out all the passion and enthusiasm you had for that business idea or plan. Something you were initially so eager to launch begins to feel like a chore. You become perpetually anxious and weary. The horror of screwing up keeps you on your toes and up at night. You carefully inspect every trivial, inconsequential detail. You are constantly editing, continual rewriting, restrategizing, redesigning until the joy disappears. Your work begins to look very stoic, void of creativity and vitality.

Time management is key. You don't have all the time in the world or resources to invest solely in one project or product. A time lost cannot be regained. Every minute you spend obsessing over details, another competitor is out there selling aggressively. Someone is launching your top-notch business idea to the world already and amassing consumers and wealth, establishing a brand name and relationship with the consumers. Your resources are limited for excessive cross-checking, trial and error. As much as you want to supply a quality product, you cannot provide the perfect one even after the excessive amount of time and resources invested. You will still have to improve and make changes. The number of resources, manpower and time left will determine the improvements you can make before someone else gets a whiff of your idea and implements it better. Time is of the essence.

Think about this. What happens if, by some magical means, we attain perfection? Will there be anything more worth fighting for? We become perfect beings. We don't need anything more to make us better, mentally, emotionally, physically or socially. If people teleport, we don't need cars. If we communicate through telepathy, we don't need phones. If we can wish anything into existence, we don't need businesses. Kids might not even need their parents. There's no growth and no challenge, just stagnant and boring perfection. Don't you hate the sounds of that? You can't stand it. This is how it sounds and looks when you say you demand or want perfect conditions, a perfect business idea, or perfect opportunity. Although it's rewarding to work hard towards success, there should always be room for growth and improvement.

Besides, the media constantly portray new images and thought patterns for the world to absorb and imitate. Get acquainted and intimate with the idea that you cannot

satisfy everyone. Initially, the perfect body was the slim body; slim tea bags sold massively. Now, the perfect body is thick and curvy. Waist trainers and plastic surgery are pushing the market. The idea is not to create an almighty product that can make people slim one minute and then make them thick and curvy the next. You should set attainable goals. Design your product or business to attend to a specific need and take action by sending it to your targeted audience as soon as it has an acceptable standard deviation. The moment it's needed is now. You can only create a quality product that appeals to your targeted consumers/customers as soon as possible. Remember, first come, first served.

Breaking The Obsession on Perfection
Breaking habits have always required a lot of patience, willingness and underlying determination. The process is quite painful but effective, and the results are visible and well-appreciated. To successfully break this cycle of perfection, we will take these nine steps in doses. Yes, it's a prescription. No, you do not have to take it all at once.

1) Outline your goals

You may decide to jot this down every morning on a to-do list as a short-term goal, or you can prepare a long-term goal list, where you can see them often. The sentences following are imperative. You may or may not complete this list. Getting eighty to ninety-five percent completed is fantastic, brilliant and commendable. You might not believe this, but I can assure you, some people in even better conditions than you haven't been able to achieve as much. So feel good about your efforts. You may decide to get yourself little trophies. This is not to make you work harder but faster. This leads us to the next pill, and trust me, they get sweeter as we go.

2) Set deadlines

I can't emphasize this enough, so I won't try to. The aim here is to motivate you to work smarter, not harder. Hence, the trophies mentioned above congratulate you on completing a bulk of the work in record time. Make sure the time frame is suitable and comfortable enough for you, not too comfortable, so you don't sneak in time for compulsive nitpicking and fault-finding.

The earlier you complete projects and goals, the faster you deliver. Launch these projects and get acquainted with the market and your target customers. The rest of the time, after your launching and completion of your projects, you can rest and clear mental cache/junk like stress and tension. You do this, and you are settled before feedback comes, and you can begin making changes and corrections with a clear head. More satisfying than anything, you feel more in control, organized and stable. You can now input more details, find faults, improve them, and relax and enjoy the outstanding outcome.

3) Two Heads Are Better Than One

You are not always right. Ask for, accept, and implement ideas from others. Even if you possess a lot of experience, it's always advisable to step back and see things differently. Taking a step back might not be enough sometimes, so you may have to take two by introducing new eyes or a couple of fresh minds. Be open to compromise, forfeiting a backward or non-functional plan, and accepting new ideas. These new ideas are not always perfect, but you can work happily and effectively with your teammates or employees to review and improve these ideas. Try not to antagonize them over minor errors and mistakes. Encourage them to share their thoughts and critiques. After all, they are also consumers and are more likely to draw out information from customers and competitors. There are better chances of success with teamwork. Teamwork makes that dream work!

4)   **Tough Love And Tough Skin**

Don't accept all criticisms and surround yourself with optimistic fellows. Trust me. You will need a good, heavy dose of their sunny disposition and good-naturedness to stop you from constantly fussing and fault-finding. Still, brace yourself for constructive and even unconstructive criticisms while having a sturdy backbone. Don't let negativity make you feel like you haven't been working hard enough or that your ideas are not good enough. As much as your critics are vital to improving your business, your advocates and appraisals remind you of how hard you have worked. The encouragement lifts your spirits and improves your work efficiency.

5)   **F. O. C. U. S**

Don't worry, it's not an acronym to start memorizing. You need to focus. The question is on what? Focus on completing most of your project, design and products and leave the editing for someone else. A perfectionist always wants to be in charge, but there is only so much you can do alone as an entrepreneur. This is one skill writers adopt that works wonders. After completing the bulk of the work, someone else does the scrutinizing, edits and rearrangements. Aside from the fact that a fresh eye is introduced, this individual can go through your work carefully without the initial boredom and drudgery you might experience if you do the work. This way, you can coordinate other managerial duties effectively.

6)   **Appropriate Authorities**

Delegate duties to your employees or teammates. That is why they work with you. Trying to do every task on your own indicates a lack of team spirit. Rather than trying to accept that some things are unattainable, let them be achieved. Let them get out of your control or grip. Allow someone else to lead. Remember, take two steps back.

7) Practice Does Not Make Perfect

You aim for improvement when you take out time to practice. However, don't expect sudden and total alignment. As the teachers say, there is always room for improvement. Trying to be perfect builds while expectations. Instead, practice being better than you were previously.

8) Prepare Forms To Get Feedback

Feedback from customers is usually our priority. If you are about to launch a new product or service, send out forms to get feedback on previous ones instead of fussing over details or worrying about what reactions you will get. If it's a new product, you can send out a questionnaire to get a general idea of what they would like and how your products will affect your targeted audience or consumers.

9) Action Is Greater Than Perfection

I have just two words: Start now! There will never be a perfect time! Okay, just one simple illustration and to end this chapter. Mrs. Nat and Mrs. Aby live in Ottawa. Both want to open a school. Mrs. Nat starts on December 1st, 2000, while Mrs. Aby waits for more people to move into the neighbourhood. She is waiting for the perfect time. Eventually, new families move in but guess where they register? You thought right, in Mrs. Nat's school and by now her school has improved, grown, and has gotten many experiences. However, her experience was not a deal-breaker. It's because she had gotten and attracted the majority of the customers available in that area. While there are some improvements to be made, she made a name and amassed a great deal of the market. **The earlier was for the better.**

My experience during COVID is a real-life example. You might ask, "how did you engineer a business during that period"? Remember what I said about the time being right? That's precisely it. It was never actually right or meant to be. I knew I had to start, or it might have never happened.

During the Mar 2020 pandemic, my Etsy shop went from 0 to 1000 sales transactions within six months.

Imperfect played a critical role that helped me generate new revenue during a pandemic.

In April, every business owner was unsure what they would do when the existing business model no longer works. Like me, my trade show business was at a halt. Luckily, I quickly identified a potential product: a social distancing floor sticker. I wasn't sure if it would work or not, since we've never done this kind of product. All the stores were closed. Only grocery stores or supermarkets were open. We didn't have any connections or clients in the retail market. Funny enough, one night, I came across the ETSY website and did some research and talked to myself. "What other sales channels do we have at this moment"? All the previous channels or strategies weren't working. I took one weekend to set up the ETSY account and start listing different variations of this product. On May 4, 2020, I launched my first product with two sizes and five different colours to choose from. On May 5, 2020,11:23am, I got my first order. I was very excited—finally, a new channel and source of revenue after a write-off a month prior.

At first, I added the floor stickers without overthinking the size, colour, combination, etc. I just did a quick listing to see what the response would be. Quickly, there was an order and feedback. I expanded from 10 SKU to 50 SKU by doing further research, with more sizes, materials, and styles. This gave me a quick and dirty way to test the market, identify the market needs, and re-design to accommodate the customer's needs.

Another idea I came across is an acrylic sneeze guard. There was a high demand for it, and I instantly jumped on the opportunity. There was very little data about customer's needs regarding this product. So, we added all the different sizes and requirements that every customer requested from us. Suppose I went back a year in time. In that case, I would not do the same, as I would have to go through the analysis, research, evaluation, research again and re-evaluation. I'd then ask my team for input and start developing the whole marketing strategy, prototype, etc. This model doesn't work now as TIME is your enemy. However, doing the above will increase your success rate with a short period of time and not enough data to do your research and evaluation. I will just have to react as quickly as possible and release what's available to the customer and determine what's needed. If I'm trying to perfect the size, decide which material to use, or which thickness of material would be best, this will slow down the whole sales process. By the time I have perfected the formula, it would be too late. Other competitors already captured the majority of the market. Long story short, if you have a specialty product and time for you to make it perfect, yes, you have the luxury to use it. In this unprecedented time, time is not on your side.

Perfection also can be viewed as your ego. In the beginning, I struggle to change my company branding because the new product doesn't fit into our existing branding. Should I start a new business name? A whole new business operation? Should I just quickly create a web page within my current company website? Of course, in the end, I decided to add a simple webpage to my website. Next, what should I call it?

Social Distancing Signage? COVID products? What are my other options? At this point, it's you who have these endless and unlimited unanswerable questions. Each question will vary in different ways, like a spider web. Prioritize what's most essential for your business and keep moving forward. Thinking out all options is good, but make sure you set a reasonable time frame or deadline.

Your mindset and habits affect not just you but your employees, teammates. If you want to bring out a quality product or offer quality service, focus on improving your work efficiency and growth instead of focusing on perfection.

Chapter 3
Planning with Time

"Complete the most important task first then tackle any other one that can be finished within 5 to 10 minutes, schedule the rest of your day accordingly, and ensure you have reachable goals."

Benjamin Franklin's famous quote, "whoever fails to plan, plans to fail," is a warning for all who seek consistent productivity in their businesses. It hints at the very essence of taking prepared steps, setting priorities, and employing discipline using strategic plans to achieve goals. For businesses, the ability to 'plan' and 'prioritize' is one way to ensure you achieve maximum output.

Planning, also known as "foresight," refers to the process of thinking about the activities required to achieve the desired goal and the procedures set out for the goal's implementation. Planning is the first step taken to ensure that you meet all goals. Prioritization on its side entails 'knowing what should come first in the face of overflowing workloads.' Different people in a business sector have various goals, many of them so wonderful that the thought of it alone makes the reality readily attainable. Mere thinking, however, does not mean that a goal is achieved, though it goes a long way into setting a pace for its actualization. This is why you should know what work you need to do first and how much time it will take to finish it. In planning, thinking comes first, setting out the thoughts in a physical aspect, and implementing these thoughts crowns it all.

In business organizations, work for a particular business owner may come in distinct pieces that often strain them. As a result of the pop-ups and their clogging, this business owner may scatter set out priorities (if one was made) or mess up an entire system's workflow. Planning is a necessary trait that every business owner should build. Lacking the ability to plan in the face of cumbersome workloads has been a threat to the productivity of every business. This has made work strenuous to organizations and often leaves them with no option but to complain all day long. As a business owner, everything suddenly seems like a top priority, and you would find yourself constantly rushing to finish different tasks all at once. It gets hard to choose what to do right away and what to do later. Some call this "mixed up priorities."

Therefore, we will need to study the importance of planning. This study also looks at some tips that will help to curtail poor planning and lack of prioritization in the face of work that needs to be done. The ones we will consider are to:

- Write down your thoughts
- List tasks according to priority
- Break more significant tasks into smaller fragments
- Practice time estimates and reality checks

WRITE DOWN YOUR THOUGHTS. When planning your tasks, it's crucial to write them down before you forget them. This way, they'll have a better chance of coming into action. Some ways you can write these thoughts down are by:

- Writing them done with a pen and paper OR
- Email yourself OR
- WhatsApp / Signal your business partner, friend, or co-worker

Writing on paper or a digital device will keep the idea alive. It acts as a reminder and has a way of connecting with the mind till you carry it out. Emailing yourself is also another strategy that helps you carry out the plans you have written down.

You can also ask your friends online to signal you. This is called 'indirect accountability.' Even if you forget or your device fails to alert you, this physical reminder will make you remember the schedule and follow it up with action. I don't like to fall behind with my schedule when someone goes to the length of reminding me. I wouldn't want to disappoint their effort, so I just do the work. But the main idea is always to get the work done!

LISTING TASKS ACCORDING TO PRIORITY. Priority means 'important". You need to list your tasks according to their 'importance.' In economics, we call this "scale of preference." One of my problems is I want to do too many things at once, and new ideas and tasks come to my mind all the time. As an entrepreneur, setting priorities is the best way to handle this and avoid starting too many tasks at a time. I currently have five employees. I overlook all different business areas, from product design, sales, accounting, graphic design, production, shipping, etc. To prioritize, I would ask the following questions;

- Are there new products that I need to add first?
- Is any associate/customer urgently waiting for a quote from me?
- Is there any invoicing that needs to be done first to get an order or get us paid faster?
- Is there an urgent deadline that needs to be executed first?
- Does any associate need my input to continue the production process?
- Is there any shipping quote or document that needs to be done first to have the order shipped out or arrive on time?
- Is there anyone that I need to schedule to speed up any process?

To set this priority right, evaluating which task needs to come first depends on what is more critical for you at the moment. Is it money, quality, customer service, or branding? Let's say I need to decide between preparing a $10,000 quote or solving a production question for a $10,000 project. For me, I would take care of the production first, as I prioritize quality over sales. Suppose the quality is not up to standard. In that case, it will jeopardize the company's reputation and will lead to fewer repeat and loyal customers. Take care of the existing customer first. Now you would ask, 'what happens if you need to prepare this quote by noon and there is a production issue at 11:30 am. Can the production issue wait for 30 minutes? How much is it going to cost you to wait? This is where you will have to refer back to chapter 2. Perfect is imperfect. There is no right or wrong to these questions. In the end, you just evaluate which is more important and carry it out first.

BREAKING BIGGER TASKS INTO SMALLER FRAGMENTS. When you have set your scale of preference, you will still need to break down the scale into smaller fragments for easy working. Eating an elephant requires gradual chopping, so does every task. With the scale at hand, find the job that requires less time and finish it first. Anything that takes less than 5 minutes should be done sooner, and the longer tasks can be done after. For tasks that take longer than 30 minutes, you should block off time for these in your calendar. This way, you ensure that the entire job gets enough time. I bring this priority mentality and 'task-fragmentalization' into play when I have a wide range of tasks that would all take different time commitments. Anyone may decide to do the challenging tasks first, but doing this may take longer than required. If the tough task is not finished, all the other functions waiting to be done will still be there.

Another example is, if I have to organize an event, say an annual workshop, it can be divided into sections. There will be a section for things that need to happen before the workshop, on the day of the workshop, and after the workshop.

For each of the sections I created, there will be a list showing one or two recurring tasks I will get done with a similar process. As I handle each of these smaller tasks, I lay a better foundation for executing a more significant task (the actual workshop day).

TIME ESTIMATES AND REALITY CHECKS. Knowing how much time it will take to complete mapped-out tasks and the workload you can handle during that time is another way of making plans that work. With time estimates, you will know exactly where to place what task. You will also know how to handle specific tasks. After all, you are the only one who knows your carrying capacity. When there is a list of priorities that you can't achieve, the brain feels less zeal for it, and with time, it gets undone. While you are trying to achieve more with less time, you should understand that making reality-check plans will always produce positive productivity. Even with all the strategies, something may go wrong, but that is not the goal. The objective is to make work easier, less stressful and yield more. You may have more than one task on your list. With the time allocated to each, you should be able to know how to go about it. From the earlier example I gave, on production and quote service, you may ask 'what happens if three things happen all at once"? My answer is simple: determine what will cost you the most.

To crown this from the 'making a list' part, here are the three scenarios:

> 1. Your supplier sends you a quote and lets you know that all the acrylics are in shortage. Everyone is buying them because of the pandemic. Now you must decide how many you would like to stock and the thickness of acrylic you will need.

2. A customer needs a sales quote for $10,000 by 4 pm. The customer already has three other bidding quotes for competitors.

3. Orders are coming in, and there is insufficient labour due to the pandemic. It's 2 pm, UPS driver comes at 4 pm, and you know 2 hours will not be enough to finish all the orders for that day.

I am using these examples because I was in this exact scenario. It needed to be done within a short time. I had to spend 5 to 10 minutes thinking about the situation. These were my thoughts.

On the material order, I was asking myself: What's the size and thickness of an acrylic sheet that I should order? What is the most popular size, and is there a need to pull sales data? Do I have enough cash? What happens if I purchase the wrong thickness? And many other questions. I spent 15 minutes and evaluated the situation, emailed back the supplier and placed an order.

On the sales quote, I had only 5 minutes to work on it. I needed to put all the remaining time into production. Finishing all the orders in my hand was more important than the quote. I copied and pasted from a previous year's quote to save time.

There was not enough time for production, so I prioritized which orders are less risky to satisfy customers. I sorted the orders by value (largest to smallest), calculated the transit time, and shipped the order that required five business days first instead of the one for local delivery. In the end, some orders were delayed, and I had to send follow-up emails to customers to provide order status updates.

With these planning methods in mind, you should also be aware of various workload problems that may arise for you and your employees.

PLANNING AND RELATED WORKLOAD PROBLEMS.

Workload issues usually come in different forms, mainly off-putting your employees. They may consist of;

- Interruptions
- Procrastination
- Repetitive processes and projects
- Changing deadlines
- Rejected projects

INTERRUPTIONS: Does this scene look familiar to you? Mr. A has to audit accounts, sign the paychecks which are already overdue, send a responding email to interns, and about two or more tasks on a working outline in a day. Now, all these are expected to be done before the workday ends at 4:00 pm. It's already 3:00 pm of these tasks that have been completed. While trying to finish these tasks, Mr. A gets a call to take his daughter to the hospital or get a text for an emergency meeting. Both require him to leave the work right away. Another scenario could be that Mr. A interrupted the power supply, which stops his work until the power is restored. There are many other examples to use.

The above scenarios delay his work and distract the employee and disrupt any laid-out plans to get the job done. Interruptions are one of the reasons employees end up achieving less. This disturbance contributes to the stagnancy of business, most times deteriorating progress to a minimal level. If you can handle interruptions and make provisions for them while still maintaining your action plan, you will achieve more productivity in your business.

PROCRASTINATION: This usually occurs when an employee feels there is plenty of time left to do their work. The employee plans their tasks but leaves them for later. Benjamin Franklin says, "you may delay, but time will not, and lost time is never found again." Why would anyone want to procrastinate anyway? Let's bring in a little science here. Behavioural Psychology uses the term "time inconsistency" to explain why you procrastinate, despite your best intentions. As Clear (2012) puts it, time inconsistency refers to the tendency of the human brain to value immediate rewards more than future rewards. Physical attributes like "stress and lack of zeal" also contribute to procrastination. Regardless, if there is work to be done, it's expected you present progressive results. Stress comes up because you have used up your energy doing other tasks, thus pushing the rest of your to-do list further away. This is why employees are instructed to include a "break period" in-between schedules (no matter how tight this might be) to replenish lost strength for another task.

A "lack of zeal" seems like something that would justify procrastination but not having the enthusiasm to start or finish a task should not be a reason for leaving it undone. Doing this affects other areas of your work. Can you imagine every employee putting off their work because they lack the zeal? Even with all the time available, very little will be achieved.

REPETITIVE PROCESSES AND PROJECTS. Doing repetitive tasks can be very dull and tiring. While it helps you learn the steps and get better with the process, it disrupts plans to achieve more. How is this possible? If you are given a task for the first time, the zeal to follow the process is always overwhelming. Through time, if the same process is needed to get your work done, you will realize that the timeframe will differ. There is less time spent as the process continues (instead of the other way round). So, almost the same result is replicated, and nothing new is obtained. So, you use more time to differentiate designs produced using the same process. The time you will need to finish different tasks gets used up in one as a consequence of these changes. Repetitive processes make it impossible to handle many tasks even when you've planned them out. Does this mean the work in question should be abandoned? Not when it's vital for the progress of other functions. It will only make sense if you develop a new method and apply it each time. Instead of starting from A-Z, try Z-A. The zeal to try new approaches will always yield good results and help you work faster.

CHANGING DEADLINES: Another issue that distorts outlined plans is "changing deadlines." Say you have been given a deadline to finish project XYZ. You make plans and map out strategies on how to complete this project within a specific time frame. Suddenly the client has changed plans, and they expect you to submit it sooner. Changing deadlines, just like 'interruptions', disorganizes you. It leaves you in a state of tension and makes the end result unattractive. Some employees may claim that they do well with deadlines, but this does not apply to 'changing deadlines.' The flow is disturbed, and you never get the best result. In situations like this, you shouldn't let your tension get the best of you. Allow yourself to take a break, then go back to look at this work with a new perspective. The purpose of the 'break' is to let the brain accept new changes and get it ready to complete what you started more effectively. Other tasks might need to be completed soon if the deadline was moved up.

REJECTED PROJECTS. No one enjoys rejections. When faced with issues like this, it might seem challenging to keep up with other tasks on your list. It affects both the employee and the work. If there are already plans made to settle other things, you end up pausing to ensure that the rejected project is reworked and approved. The time you spend on this should be spent on something else, but the others will have to wait because the work needs to be done. The employee's psychology is affected by this rejection. They wonder about what next step to take and if that will also be rejected. Time gets shortened, and less is produced.

When you consider these obstacles, and the solutions I have laid out for you, planning will become easier. You will achieve things with less stress and more accuracy if you keep these setbacks in mind.

Chapter 4
Build A Mind That Sequence Multitask

"There are many small tasks that need to be done every day. Micro-tasks are always complicated, but you know you have to do them. Just set the most optimized path and finish it."

There may be a time where you have a list of tasks to complete that you can quickly complete simultaneously. You may be able to read, type, and create voice notes for a class all at the same time. Suppose you've allocated separate times for each task. Do you wait until you finish reading before moving on when you know you can juggle the three tasks simultaneously? The ability to easily switch between tasks is known as "multitasking."

Suppose you want to improve in your field. In that case, the ability to multitask and "planning," which we discussed in the previous chapter, is one of the fundamental things you need to build. Many people think that the word "multitasking" means doing too much simultaneously. This is not always the case. If you have trouble writing stories (which can be very difficult), you wouldn't expect to juggle "writing" and "taking voice notes. Both require heavy mental processing. A delay in one of these tasks is detrimental to the other. The "speed and accuracy" in productivity is what everyone is looking for. When this is lacking, the goal is not achieved. Using an approved definition, "multitasking" refers to switching from one activity to another so quickly that it feels like working on multiple things at once. When you can effortlessly do different things simultaneously, the result we get is positive because more is achieved.

There are many other examples of multitasking. You could be preparing several orders at once for a meeting; serving drinks to a customer, providing paper information to another; preparing a sales presentation while receiving a complaint from a customer; washing and spreading simultaneously.

DO WE NEED TO MULTITASK IN ALL CONDITIONS?

The answer is NO. There are times when you shouldn't try to "multitask." It could lead to wasted time. Although it's possible to switch between functions, don't multitask under the following conditions;

1. **When the work is bulky and requires total attention.** Every job requires your attention, but there are exceptional jobs that require more time and experience. For example, if you have paperwork to do for a client and other tasks to do, instead of switching between them, you introduce "prioritization." Perform the most urgent task first and build your construction comfortably. If the paperwork is more significant than the other task, you can do the paperwork first and then do the task later. If you try to do these two together, you might spoil the construction or do the wrong thing altogether. It would be best if you only multitasked for minor tasks that are manageable. You should not flaunt that 'multi-tasker tag' when you need to do a better job with all your focus. You should be aware of the tasks on your list that require more attention and handle them separately.

2. **As a new entrepreneur, learn the ropes first:** If you just started your business, you need to understand the steps involved. You shouldn't try to juggle between jobs that you're not familiar with. Many individuals try to cut corners and end up disappointed. You might ask, "who would cut corners as a new business"? There are cases where poorly made end-products result from trying to ' do them together ' or to ' finish on time.' After you've learned the basic principles of the job, you can efficiently juggle smaller tasks simultaneously without issues.

Multi-tasking is simple but can also have drawbacks. This should not scare you. Once you learn what these drawbacks are, it will help you avoid them. Let's take a stroll.

DRAWBACKS OF MULTITASKING

There will always be negatives to every positive. In my year's experience as a business owner, I noticed these disadvantages of multitasking:

1. Divided Attention
2. Heightened Stress
3. Error tendency

    1. **DIVIDED ATTENTION.** When you have to juggle multiple tasks simultaneously, there is a chance that you will not be focused enough on each job. You should familiarize yourself with the difficulties in staying focused. This means that as a business owner, you will have to forgo the attachment you have to a specific task. For example, if I was paying close attention to the reading of a clock to report its movement, and at the same time have to write a long note stating how these clocks, instead of enjoying the movement of the clock, I will have to focus on 'observation of movement' and making my long note. So, because my mind is not focused on one thing, some of these other benefits that come with a task are sacrificed. Divided attention comes with baggage of its own. If you have not built discipline, you might get overly distracted and misplace one thing against another.

    2. **HEIGHTENED STRESS.** Carrying out one task consumes energy. Therefore, when you're doing multiple tasks at once, the stress will increase. You tend to have a diminished cognitive ability when there are too many

jobs to do. You can use a smartphone that on 'minimize mode' to check this example out. When you have many applications running simultaneously on your device, it lags or malfunctions. When a human handles more tasks simultaneously, both physical and mental abilities are affected like the smartphone—some resort to taking drugs to correct this, while others break down for a while. A business owner is advised to choose a proportioned amount of work at a time for a better result.

3. **ERROR TENDENCY.** One of the things you should bear in mind while multi-tasking is that errors will occur (noticeable or not). The more experience you have juggling your work tasks, the fewer errors you'll make. This is why some employ the use of auxiliary apps and tools to make fewer mistakes. Even when doing one task at a time, mistakes can be made, but the case is heightened when doing multiple tasks at a time. As a business owner, you need to know your capability and how much you can handle at a time. Once, an employee had multiple tasks on her plate, so she turned in poorly typed work. I told her that instead of producing shoddy work and have other poorly done tasks to follow, why not focus on one so that others will fall in place? This is the problem. While you try to get everything done and beat deadlines, know that errors might pop up. If it's not handled well, it will spoil things for the employee and the employer.

Keeping these drawbacks of multitasking in mind, business owners can make it easier and more effective. The following section below will address this.

HOW TO MULTITASK BETTER

There is no simple way of multi-tasking, but there are ways to make the process easier and faster. These methods proposed have been affirmed by people who employed them in their day-to-day lives. Utilizing and studying these will help the mind relax and work effectively. Some of the ones I'll consider here include:

1. Using apps and split-work devices
2. Using to-do lists
3. Scaling a preference list
4. Grouping tasks
5. Delegation
6. Practice

1. **USE OF APPLICATIONS AND SPLIT-WORK DEVICES.** The world has become digitized. There are plenty of applications and devices designed to help you handle multiple tasks simultaneously. So, instead of doing little tasks separately, you can easily use an app and complete them all. This, however, depends on the type of work. Some of the applications are already on our smartphones. Every smartphone has been designed to have a 'minimize' function. As a social media manager, while waiting to respond to emails and reply to chats, you will only need to minimize your apps to respond to your clients. Some smartphones use already prepared apps with attributes. For example, suppose all available personnel are engaged with other functions in a customer care station. In that case, an operator keeps you company or gives you the required information a human resource employee would have provided you. For business analysts, there is the 'multi-tasking operating system (MOS).' For stay-at-home moms, there is the laundry machine, the blender, and other devices that help you accomplish multiple tasks at once.

2. **USE OF TO-DO LISTS:** Using to-do lists will help

you multitask better. All you need to do is jot down the tasks you need to complete on paper or in a notepad. You may have already written down similar jobs, helping you choose whether to do them together or not. When I want to achieve more, I try to write down everything I need to do in a day before carrying them out. I check each task and tick it off at the end of the day. When I go back to the list, most times, I find out that I finished everything.

When I have a task that needs to be completed, with multiple minor tasks involved, I'll write them all done, so I don't forget. For example, if I need to print a retractable banner, I know I also have to prepare the banner stand, cross tools, and supplies and clean the warehouse before starting the trimming and installation of the banner stand. Having all these written down means I can quickly remind myself what I have left to do.

3. **USE A SCALE OF PREFERENCE LIST:** Some may want to call this "setting a priority list." The word 'SEQUENCE' used in this Chapter's title refers to the orderly arrangement of tools according to importance. Since not being able to set priorities is one of the disadvantages of multi-tasking, it would be advisable to learn to set your tasks according to priority. Like I already advised, put the easy-to-be-finished ones at the top and finish them up and look at the importance of knowing which should come first on your list. The less important ones can wait for later or be removed. I'm pretty sure the majority of business owners have some level of multi-tasking. Here is how I evaluate myself when it comes to working. I ask:

- Am I optimizing and managing similar tasks?

- When I need to pick up an item from one vendor, am I picking up everything else that I need for today and tomorrow, or even this week?

- If I'm going to vendor #1 to pick up an order, are there other supplies that I need to go to in the same area?

- If the items that I need are not urgent, can I consolidate with another delivery/order to optimize the route?

These help me place orders according to their importance and ensure I carry them out efficiently.

4. **GROUPING TASKS.** Grouping in multi-tasking means working on similar tasks together to make things easier. As a business owner, you can group smaller tasks using the same method. This helps you work effectively and faster. You get stressed and find tasks challenging, especially when there are too many at a time, but you can switch focus back and forth if you can work on similar jobs at a time. For example, suppose there are 20 posts you need to share on multiple social media accounts. In that case, you can group them and use the 'minimize function' to submit them to the different handles. Knowing that some tasks look alike and can be handled all at once will help your mind relax and cross something else off your 'to-do list.'

5. **DELEGATION.** You might wonder if asking someone else to do part of your job is a way of improving 'multitasking.' Delegation can help you get a job done faster. If buying labour can help you finish a task quicker and more efficiently, why wait to finish one strenuous task before moving to the other? The delegation of functions has helped many organizations improve. People who employ other people to handle distinct job positions improve multitasking because the work gets done faster. Delegation does not mean that you, as a business owner,

should be lazy. People tend to depend on others to get their work done, but this is not the point we are trying to make. We emphasize distributing these functions if there are too many tasks and one person can't handle them all. It's a bid to help get more things done. For people outside the business industry, you have stay-at-home moms hiring house cleaners to help make their roles easier. This lightens the wife's workload. She will now have time to focus on other aspects of her home.

6. **KEEP PRACTICING.** Practice will always make perfect. To get better at something, the only way to improve is to practice consistently. Multi-tasking is a skill that requires practice before you can master it. I always tell my staff to optimize their workflow. I ask them to finish all the work as fast as they can but never to cut corners. Cutting corners usually have a way of coming back to haunt you. When getting all tasks done before the deadline, feel free to take breaks. Procrastinating tasks to do less work and hoping others will help you finish tasks is not acceptable. Therefore, be prepared to complete your task by using all resources available. When the time comes, you could have developed a set routine to be a multi-tasker. Multi-tasking is a must in small businesses, even with the environment, labour, and resources as a limitation. Everyone is expected to work 200% when the rush hour comes.

In conclusion, prepare yourself and your staff to be ready for the rush. Some of the best examples of multi-taskers are restaurant employees, hospital personnel, and working/full-time Moms. I am not in this industry, but I am sure anyone can imagine. Here are some ways these professions require multitasking:

- Restaurant employees work during breakfast, lunch, and dinner, each taking a 2-3 hour time slot. This could cause a lot of stress. If you have not mastered multitasking, I believe you couldn't handle this kind of job.

- Hospital staff have just a split second between life and death. The pressure is on in this career, and sufficient training is a must. Again, if you are not a multi-tasker, you might be able to handle this role.

- Moms have the most challenging responsibilities in the world. They take care of kids, husbands, family members, office employees, and an endless list of unlimited tasks. They need to learn to multitask at home, as well as in their careers.

There is something common among all the multi-sequencing taskers. They all have excellent time management skills. We will talk about this in the next Chapter. Knowing how to multitask and putting it into practice can go a long way in helping you function effectively and achieve your business goals.

Chapter 5
Time Management with different skills and tools

"Few of us accomplish what we truly want because we never direct our concentration; we never focus our power. Most people dabble their way through life and never decide to master anything in particular."

What is Time?

I don't want to sound all philosophical but let's look at this definition.

"Time is something that we experience daily, characterized by notions such as the past, present and the future. Its progression is embodied in our continued experience of the future becoming the present, while the present becomes the past." - Qmahdi Godazgar (2016).

Time is an unstoppable force of nature; it flows and keeps running no matter what. It's a wonderful asset allocated to everyone. However, it always seems like there's never enough of it.

With so many activities clogging our day, it would appear that there is never enough time. I find it strange, though, we all get 24 hours, but there's always one colleague who seems to achieve so much more with their time than others. The reason lies in good time management.

For someone in the workspace, every second is valuable. That's one of the reasons we have deadlines, quarterly reports, and off-days. Time is an asset we can't control but can manage. The highest performers in any organization have mastered time management. By acquiring time management skills, you can improve your ability to beat deadlines, outperform others, and have still have time to kick back, relax and binge on Netflix.

According to Wikipedia, time management involves planning

and exercising conscious control of time spent on some activities, especially to maximize effectiveness, efficiency, and productivity.

As the above definition states, time management requires a conscious shift in focus from being busy to producing results. Why? Simply because being busy doesn't necessarily mean you are effective.

Being busy means spending your day plowing through various activities and achieving less. Being productive requires allocating time to each task and acting on them based on importance and urgency.

With definitions out of the way, how do you manage time effectively?

Let's look at something called the Priority Matrix.

There are many self-help books and YouTube videos on this subject. Before we delve into the various ways to manage our time, let's start with the basics.

You may have heard of the Priority Matrix, but I'll give you a brief background just in case. Dwight David Eisenhower was the 34th United States President from 1953 to 1961. He was responsible for scheming an allied invasion against Europe as a supreme commander during the Second World War in the United States Army.

As President, he continuously made difficult conclusions about what tasks to focus on and which ones to delegate. He created a method consisting of 4 Quadrants:

    i. Urgent and important.
    ii. Urgent but not important.

iii. Not urgent but important.

iv. Not urgent and not important.

The method he created enabled him to prioritize tasks. It later became known as the Eisenhower Method or Priority Matrix.

So that's it for history class. I'll be expecting a report from you by the end of this book. Just kidding!

Entrepreneur's who have applied this method prioritize better, beat deadlines, and manage distractions (we'll talk more about this in the next chapter). You can also utilize this method to delegate tasks and attend to matters based on urgency and importance.

Now that we've defined the Priority Matrix, let's take a look at how it works.

	Urgent	Not urgent
Important	Q1. Have important deadlines with high urgency. They need immediate action and should be attended to immediately	Q2. Are important but with a low level of urgency. Long-term strategies are usually found in this quadrant.
Not Important	Q3. They are unimportant but have a high level of urgency. This could be a distraction from setting goals, and delegation is recommended in this case.	Q4. They are unimportant and not urgent; they don't yield any input and should be eliminated.

Look at the above table; you see a basic breakdown of how the matrix works.

Let's take a deeper look.

> Q1 (Urgent and important): I'm sure you have a basic idea of how this works based on the title. Tasks that fall in this quadrant deserve special attention and focus. If not, there would be many consequences. Let's look at an example.

Let's say you work as an intern for a ghostwriting startup. Your supervisor tells you to write a 3,000-word report for a client by the end of the day.

Just by observing the delivery time, you can tell how important and urgent the project is. Your full attention is required for activities in this quadrant and usually only takes a single day to complete.

> Q2 (Not urgent but important): This quadrant consists of long-term goals and essential tasks that don't have an immediate deadline.

For example, if you were given the same 3,000-word report to do, but you have a two-week deadline instead.

It would be advisable to break the task into smaller tasks and work on one each day. That way, you focus on other duties while still having enough time to complete the long-term ones.

> Q3 (Urgent but not important): These tasks, although unimportant, have a high level of urgency. The best way to handle tasks in this quadrant would be to delegate. It's essential to keep track of the tasks you have delegated. Without proper monitoring and feedback, these jobs can slip through the cracks and not get done. It's best to

finish working on Q1 and Q2 tasks before focusing on this quadrant.

Q4 (Not Urgent, not important): These are things that don't relate to your work at all. Checking personal emails, social media, or playing on your smartphone during work hours are examples of these kinds of tasks. Take good care to ensure that you don't fall victim to these distractions.

Using the priority matrix to plan, prioritize, delegate, and schedule your tasks, you will see that you can utilize your time effectively, achieve your goals and become more productive.

Now that you have a basic idea of how the priority matrix works let's explore various ways you can beat deadlines by managing your time effectively.

1. Parkinson's Law – The following scenario may be familiar to you. Let's say you have a task that you plan to complete by 4:30 pm. Typically the task takes two hours to complete, but you want to take your time to ensure you get it done perfectly. Now it takes longer to get the task done because you're spending time doing busy work.

This typically happens with tasks that fall under the second quadrant in the Priority Matrix. Parkinson's Law states that tasks tend to consume the time allocated to them. Try creating stricter deadlines. That way, you can cut off the time consumption and emphasize what is most important. Additionally, you can make 60-90 minute deadlines to complete specific tasks. Please take it as therapy that forces you to utilize your time wisely.

2. The 80/20 Rule – You've probably heard about the Pareto Principle, which suggests that 80% of work outputs result from 20% of inputs. This principle can be applied to tasks

in the second quadrant of the Priority Matrix. Focus on the 20%, which serves as a starting point or an outline to the project and fill out the other 80% later. Authors use this principle before writing a book. They prepare a summary of each chapter.

3. Hofstadter's Law – This law states that it will always take longer than you'd expect. When dealing with tasks from the first quadrant, it's advisable to double the amount of time you think you need. Observe how long it usually takes you to complete similar tasks and double that time. You can use that extra time to go over your work again, reducing the number of mistakes in the finished product.

4. Experiment – The best way to become better at quickly producing results is to practice. Just like athletes practice to increase their performance time or perfect their skills, entrepreneurs can do the same. When attempting something new, test out smaller versions of a project to help you decide on a final deadline. Write a 10-page ebook before a 300-page novel, or try to increase your income by 10% before aiming to double it.

5. Observe the downsides – What could go wrong? Be sure to identify this. It's easy to assume that you've got it all figured out, and completing your tasks will be as easy as a walk in the park. There's one thing life has constantly made us aware of, and things won't always go the way you expect. Before starting a task, find out what could go wrong and identify ways to prevent that from happening.

6. Avoid impossible deadlines – Remember you are human. You need to know when to hit the brakes. Using the first quadrant isn't an excuse to work for sixteen hours straight. It's not a good idea; it's unhealthy and a waste of valuable time.

7. Feedback – Remember when I said you should run experiments? Feedback is a similar principle. You can gauge your productivity level from those in your immediate circle. Never be too scared or proud to ask your teammates to evaluate you. Constructive criticism will help you identify your weaknesses, improve your growth and build your confidence.

8. Continuous planning – If you use a backward planning model, you need to constantly update your plans to suit your deadlines. Backward planning involves making cuts, additions, or refinements to fit the project into the expected timeframe. Consider how you handled a previous project that you completed on time. What mistakes did you make that delayed a delivery? Ask yourself these questions and continuously update your current task delivery.

9. Avoid baggage – Identify areas of a task or project that will not get completed if you run out of time. In the second quadrant of the Priority Matrix, we dealt with not important and not urgent tasks. Ask yourself what emails you need to respond to right now and which ones can wait until later. Which of your colleagues needs your assistance urgently and which ones can wait? If it's not urgent, leave it for now and focus on more critical tasks.

10. Review – For deadlines under the second quadrant in the Priority Matrix, which are usually long-term, it's essential to document weekly reviews that will help track your progress. Think of it as personal feedback that will help you identify methods you can use to speed up tasks and help you plan more efficiently for the future.

11. Take the easier path – Every task or project can be done in more efficient ways. If you have predecessors, do you have templates you can use to get them done quicker? Are there

sample reports you can access online? How about an auto-responder to answer similar emails? Is there a professional you can call upon to help solve your problems? You don't have to reinvent the wheel, especially when dealing with tasks that have a high level of urgency and importance.

12. Churn then polish – Set a strict deadline for essential tasks and then set a more comfortable deadline to enhance and polish your work afterwards.

13. Reminders – Haunt yourself. Post reminders of your deadlines everywhere. You can do this with sticky notes on your PC, jotting them down in your journal, or using a Google Calendar. This way, you create an atmosphere of urgency, which is necessary to keep deadlines from being pushed aside by distractions. Setting a timer (one that beep) can also be helpful. The countdown of a timer is more beneficial than just glancing at your clock. Don't use your phone for this if it's going to be a distraction. Be sure also to write down the tasks you need to complete. Any deadline that exceeds an hour needs to be written down. Otherwise, it's no longer a goal. Writing deadlines makes them more tangible compared to just making internal decisions.

14. Forward Planning *Not mutually exclusive with backward planning* – This involves planning the project's details before creating a task with an urgent deadline. This helps in achieving clarity about what you are trying to accomplish before making absolute time limits.

Now you have a concept of how time management works and how to manage your time more efficiently. It will surprise you that you have more free time than you think!

In the next chapter, we'll be handling a significant challenge to effective time management: **Distractions.**

Chapter 6
Manage Distraction - Not to AVOID it

"Successful people maintain a positive focus in life no matter what is going on around them. They focus on their past success rather than their past failures. They concentrate on the next action steps to fulfil their goals rather than on other distractions that life presents."

We all get distracted. It's an unavoidable part of our lives. I'll bet you $5 that you got distracted by family, friends, or social media while reading this book.

The funny thing is that distractions always happen when we are focused on doing significant work. Here are two examples:

1. Say, for instance, you are a graphics design intern, and your supervisor has requested you create a new brand logo for the organization. This is a big opportunity! If this goes well, you could get a wage increase or become a full-time staff member with lots of benefits. The only problem is, you don't have any ideas. Not to worry, the internet was made for stuff like this. You search Google and find a site with 'sample ideas for designing a brand logo.' You read through the site and don't seem to find what you're looking for. Under 'suggested articles,' you see 'top Instagram handles you need to follow as a graphic designer.' Even though you swore you wouldn't check your social media, you convince yourself that it's for work and open Instagram anyway. After checking out the handles, you decide you can spare a few more minutes before heading back to work—big mistake. You get caught up scrolling through feeds and eventually lose track of time.

2. Let's say you're a supervisor and given an important task to update the company's financial records before 3 pm. It's noon now, and so far, so good. Your phone is tucked away, and you're in the zone. All of a sudden, there's a knock on your office door. A graphic design intern, who you asked to develop a new brand logo for the organization, is in a rut and has no idea what to do. The logo doesn't have to be

finished until the end of the month, but you don't want the intern to stay idle. You both look at past design ideas until he understands what you're looking for. The time is now 1 pm but don't worry, you'll make it, or so you think. Another intern is at the door, and you don't want to turn her away.

There are plenty of examples that show how we face distractions in the workplace. Some of these distractions we have no control over. There will always be long boring meetings, interns who need our help, requests from co-workers, social media, or bosses that pile more work on your lap. It's challenging to stay industrious and get the job done with all these things in the way. Distractions lower our output and cost us time.

You can't avoid distractions entirely, but you can manage them.

Before we get into how they can be managed, let's identify some of the ways distractions occur.

Colleagues. We all have different types of co-workers. We're encouraged to build relationships with them to increase our network and professional life. Among them is what I like to call '**The office gossip**.' The office gossip always seems to have the best stories. Time flies when talking to him or her. Whether this is a good thing or a bad thing depends on the situation. Say, for example, you have a deadline, and he/she engages you in a conversation. It's a juicy one about the colleague you're interested in. Now that's tempting, no?

Another type of co-worker that can cause distractions is the junior staff. They require your assistance to get work done when you also have a deadline. If you are always available, you'll be required to answer multiple questions, which infringes on your productivity.

How do you manage this?

When dealing with *'the office gossip,'* the logical thing would be to have a conversation with him/her and let them understand the effect it's having on your day. Don't be rude or say, *"Dammit, Jerry, back off! I'm trying to work here!"* Instead, you could say, *"That's awesome stuff, Jerry. Tell you what, let me just finish up with this, and then we can go for some drinks and finish this conversation. Better not leave anything out."*

When dealing with interns or junior staff, let them know that you are currently occupied and will assist them later.

Lastly, it would be best to determine when to say 'No.' We will discuss this further in Chapter 7.

Meetings: We all hate them, especially the ones that have your boss repeating the same thing over and over again for almost an hour. Don't forget about the complaints they have about the meetings being too long because your team doesn't deliver or that you should have the organization at heart. *"Fine, we get it; can we wrap this up already?"* Trust me, we've all been there. As a business owner, the last thing you would want to do is have long meetings, especially unproductive ones, with your junior employees or staff.

'Overall, 31 hours are spent in unproductive meetings over an average month, with 91% of employees guilty of daydreaming, while 39% have admitted to falling asleep' – Atlassian.com *(You waste a Lot of Time at Work).*

As a business owner, you might wonder, *"How are meetings a distraction? I'm only ensuring everyone knows what to do."* Well, there's nothing wrong with meetings, but the hours spent talking about practically nothing is a significant distraction.

If your junior staff come fired up and raring to go in the morning and you make them sit still listening to you lecture them for hours, it will disorient their day.

How do you manage this?

First things first, make the meetings short! Have a clear plan on how the meetings should go, important matters to discuss, and a call to action.

I recommended starting the meeting on a positive note by getting everyone in the room to share highlights of the previous week, emphasizing the things they could accomplish.

There's no need to meet every day of the week. Meetings could be held every Monday, Wednesday and Friday. Monday meetings could have a clear schedule for the week and determine a leader who will be accountable for the week's affairs. Each of the team members will be assigned tasks according to their abilities and output levels. Wednesday could be a progress report meeting. Those who were assigned tasks will give feedback, ask for input and make adjustments. Friday could be for final assessments. This example is just a suggested meeting schedule. You can use whatever schedule suits your organization best.

Noise. You might not be friends with '*the office gossip*,' but that doesn't stop him or her from talking. During your career, you might have observed how noisy working in a big office can be. This can be attributed to the loud colleague who can't seem to make a phone call without raising his/her voice, the one colleague who doesn't know to use the *'vibrate only'* function on their smartphone, or the one who doesn't like using headphones.

Sadly, you aren't the only one with this problem.

According to an investigation done by Jungsoo Kim and Richard de Dear from the University of Sydney, 30% of staff who work in partitions and 25% of those who didn't were uncomfortable with noise levels at work. Not only that, research from Ipsos and the Workspace Futures Team of Steelcase determined 85% of people can't concentrate in their workspace due to noise.

How do you manage this?

If you have a private office, the best course of action would be closing the door. By doing this, you are letting your colleagues know you want some privacy. If you don't want to keep the door permanently closed, you can simply close it when the noise level increases. This lets your colleagues know they are too loud.

When you are dealing with '*the office gossip*' or co-workers who talk loudly on the phone or don't place their phones on vibrate, you could have a quiet conversation about how their noise levels affect your work.

Working away from your desk, if possible, can also be helpful. Say you have an important project to work on, and you need as much silence as you can get. Try finding a quiet space within your office complex where you can work seamlessly. Another alternative is to work from home. Only do this if you can work effectively from home. You could also try working from another location such as a library, park or café.

The truth is you can't eradicate noise in an office. Trust me, it will become unbearable at some point in time. When you have important work to do, change your environment to one more suitable to aid your focus.

Distracting websites. Remember the first example where we discussed social media? The internet is a fantastic place to help find resources to make your job easier. There's nothing wrong with using it efficiently. The trouble starts when you get caught in the *'Suggested Articles'* part of the web. This usually happens after we convince ourselves that we still have plenty of time to get back our work done, which we all know is a lie.

How do you manage this?

Discipline plays a key role in managing this particular distraction. As I explained earlier, searching for materials that would assist your job isn't a bad thing. However, you need to ensure you don't stray from the task you have visited the site for. Grab what you want and hightail it out of there!

If you lack willpower, you could try using some website blocking tools that prevent you from visiting certain websites during work hours. Here's a list of some options:

1. Limit (a Chrome extension)
2. StayFocused (a Chrome extension)
3. WasteNoTime (a Chrome and Safari extension)
4. LeechBlock (a Mozilla Firefox extension)

Emails. Let's go over another example, shall we?

You have yet to finish the brand logo your boss has asked for, and now he has sent you an email requesting your immediate attention. He's instructed you to address the email and then get back to work on the logo. You finish the task in the email, and since you're already in your emails, you wonder if you should check your personal ones as well.

Let's pause there for a moment. You might be guilty of this situation. One minute you're fully engaged with your work, then you open an email to send an update to your boss, and you convince yourself to view your inbox. Often the emails are entirely unrelated to your current job. You are faced with two choices: either stop what you're doing to check your email, or stay disciplined and read your emails on your break or at the end of the workday.

I should mention that breezing through emails will create an atmosphere of busyness rather than productivity and will often lead to incomplete tasks at the end of the day.

How do you manage this?

Discipline! I can't spell it out enough. Using the scenario mentioned above as a case study, be sure to resist the urge to review your personal emails. It's easier said than done, but it can be done.

There are other ways you can manage Email usage;

1) **Avoid checking personal emails first thing in the morning.** We have fallen victim to this lots of times. We check our emails as soon as we wake up in the morning or get into the office. It's not a bad idea to stay abreast of matters or current events, but ask yourself, *"is it really a good idea to start my day like this?"* Rather than logging into Gmail first thing in the morning, the advisable thing would be to focus on significant tasks for the day. Your emails can wait until break periods.

2) **Work offline.** Pop-ups from notification assistants only appear when your computer is connected to a network. When those notifications appear, you will be tempted to view them. It's best to work offline. Before you come up with the excuse that you would need the internet to research materials for work, I have a suggestion. Download every resource you need the night so you can work offline the

following day. Don't worry about receiving a new email. Allow the messages to stay in your inbox until you're ready to review. Responding to emails in batches also consumes less time than reacting to them individually. This method allows you room to complete important tasks without being distracted.

3) **Finally, set out specific times to review emails.** Just because you aren't supposed to check personal email during work hours doesn't mean you have to ignore your email entirely. All you have to do is set up specific times you'll need to review emails. You can do it in the morning while on the bus to work, during lunch breaks, or the final hour before work is over to ensure you're in the loop. If you want to apply this method, it would be prudent to create 'out-of-office' response messages.

Social media and smartphone usage. Finally, the big one. In this day and age, our smartphones and social media influence most of our daily routines. It's the first thing we look at in the morning. It's where we get our steady supply of dopamine through the number of likes and reposts we get, and for most of us, it's our best friend.

It's important to remember that while there's nothing wrong with checking your notifications or clearing Level 1898 on Candy Crush, using your phone or scrolling through your feed during work hours causes a breakdown in your workflow and focus.

Research shows that the average person checks their phone at least 47 times a day. Translating that to an 8-hour workday means you're on your phone at least six times every working hour! I don't know about you, but that's an awful lot of time you could be using to be productive at work.

For social media, be honest; how much time do you spend scrolling through feeds during work hours? Let's do a quick experiment:

Download Moment (available on iOS and Android) it's an app that tells you how much time you spend on apps. If you use an iPhone, you might be aware of **'Screen Time,'** a built-in feature that monitors your app usage. Don't look at your daily average, as it considers email and other work-related phone usages. Check your list of "Most Used" apps. Now, how much time do you spend on social media?

While you read this book, some of your co-workers are probably scrolling through their phones. You might have even closed this book a few times to scroll through your phone as well.

It's not a bad thing. With catalogues of information, memes, and DIY posts out there, you can't help but want to check them all out.

How do you manage this?
Let me break this down into simple tasks you can accomplish:

    i.   **Move your phone.** You can't be tempted by what you can't see. Some offices have a protocol where everyone turns in their phones at the front desk and only has access to them at the end of the day. If your office doesn't do this, you could try turning off your notifications, placing your phone in a drawer, or keeping it out of reach. This way, you won't be curious enough to take a peek.

    ii.   **Disable most used social media apps.** Alright, before you panic, disabling apps doesn't mean you are deleting them permanently. You are just deactivating them for at least 8 hours. You can easily enable them again after you have finished the workday. This is purely experimental as it's meant to test how you react to not being on social media and how productive you become without it.

iii. **Have an accountability partner:** It can be easier to limit the distraction of social media during work hours by asking someone to keep you accountable. Identify a colleague who is interested in managing his or her social media addiction as well. You both can exchange phones during work hours. That way, you can both focus on work rather than wondering how many likes you have on your new post.

Always remember, you can't wholly avoid distractions, but you can manage them. Make meetings short, avoid scrolling during work hours, respond to emails at specific times, and keep your phone out of reach.

You're on your way to managing distractions like an efficient business owner.

Chapter 7
Learn To Say 'Yes' When It Is A 'No'

"Saying 'NO' is hard, especially to your favourite customer. That is why you must learn the act of saying "yes" even when the answer should be the negation."

This is going to be challenging but worth it. Learning to say "Yes" when the answer is "No" is something you need to cultivate. It has worked for me over the years, and I have gotten better at many things just by doing it.

WHY I SHOULD SAY 'YES' WHEN THE ANSWER IS 'NO'

Some reviews on this strategy have been done. Here is some reason why you should say 'yes' when you want to say 'no':

- **When you say 'yes,' you learn more**
- **It keeps you in business**
- **It saves your reputation**
- **It changes how you think**
- **It tests your capability**

WHEN YOU SAY 'YES,' YOU LEARN MORE. You probably wonder why saying 'yes' aids in learning. We have lots of opportunities presented to us in our distinct life pursuits. When we take them on (which is worth doing), not all will yield positive results. When you agree to take on new opportunities that present themselves to you, you give your mind the openness to learn more. Say, for example, you are interested in writing. You're trying to make some extra money, and someone offers you a teaching job. The teaching job should only last one session, but you will earn the extra money you're looking for. Should you not accept the offer, since your goal is to make some extra income? I guess you would need to prepare lesson notes, make a lesson plan, and practice public speaking to ensure that you do a good job. This medium is applied to other opportunities that may present themselves to you on your career journey. They help you expand your knowledge.

As an entrepreneur, saying "yes" more often can help expand your productivity and work efficiency. Constantly saying "no" can kill possible achievements. You won't know how things will work out until you try them. This is why you need to accept some of the offers that come your way. It doesn't mean that you have to say "yes" to everything, though. Suppose you have no interest in the job or lack the skills to complete it. That is when your true 'NO' comes in. For example, someone who offers legal services cannot abandon it entirely to do a Cobbler's job.

IT KEEPS YOU IN BUSINESS. When you reject the offers that come your way because you feel there are some other works to finish, you might disappoint some good-paying clients. This is never wise for anyone who understands business ethics and wishes to grow. Saying 'yes' makes it easier to retain your paying customers. It builds a certain level of trust in them, helps you develop expertise in your skill, and assures them of your delivery time. If you want to be successful, don't say 'no' before considering its effect on your business. A friend of mine told me about a time he lost one of his good-paying clients to another contractor. The client had called him to get a service done, but because he didn't feel up to it when the offer came in, he rejected it. The client found another contractor to do the work. The other contractor also got the job done for a cheaper rate. My friend lost this customer for life. If he had just said 'yes,' checked out the job, and delegated it to another contractor, he wouldn't have lost the client. The customer wouldn't have been forced to hire a competing contractor.

IT SAVES YOUR REPUTATION. Imagine having to shut down your business because of a lack of customers and no positive review. Your reputation isn't just about offering good products. Your ability to say 'yes' even when you indirectly throw back a 'no' can save your business. I accept offers from clients, and when I can't get the work done, I increase the prices of my services even when I know the client might not pay that price. I don't approach this directly. I employ some strategies and get the problem solved. Don't consider this deceit. You'll protect yourself and your business from numerous issues if you understand how this method works. Make it clear when you cannot help it; it will be evident to the client, who will know that it's not your fault. They may even be pushed into sentimental consideration, but you have to play your part well.

IT CHANGES HOW YOU THINK. Saying 'yes' helps you change your mindset on approaching new opportunities. You will see possibility in every endeavour that comes your way. As I already mentioned, you don't have to accept every offer on the table. Still, you don't have to reject things that are new to you. Top entrepreneurs didn't make it to the top in one day. They utilized prospects. They didn't do that by saying 'no' to taking chances. They continued to try new things because they saw the advantages of saying "yes." New ideas birthed new developments and sustaining levels of achievement. You can try the same too. The act of accepting new challenges helps you see more opportunities, whether beautiful or ugly. But like I said before, don't accept every new offer that comes your way. It's the difference between expanding your horizons and running yourself into the ground. Some authors call this "burning bright and burning out" (Hutchins, 2012).

IT TESTS YOUR CAPABILITY. Sometimes, when I accept a banner-printing job for a client, I take on more than I can handle. It helps me test my limits. When I fill my printer at 99% productivity in a day, I get more stressed than when it's just working at 50%. How did I learn this? I test myself by accepting more (saying yes) when I know I cannot handle the workload.

Someone who intends to get the best out of themselves should test their limits. You might be surprised at what you discover. Strengths vary, and you won't know how much you can carry on if you don't put yourself to the test. See accepting offers as a way of stretching yourself, testing new waters, and obtaining better results. Some entrepreneurs also find it hard to reject offers. Taking on a more significant workload can help you understand how far you can go. Knowing that disappointing a client might cost you, you will try new rejecting steps by accepting. It's a two-way street. You get to turn the job down but still retain your business and your name.

I repetitively reminded you that you don't have to say 'yes' to everything. I highlighted some examples where 'no' is the right answer. Entrepreneurs generally have ways of choosing what they say 'yes' or 'no' to. Let's look at some ways to help you decide which answer to choose.

ENTREPRENEURS DECISION ON WHAT TO SAY 'YES' TO

These should be taken under the following;

- Prospect Consideration
- Profit Consideration
- Comfort Consideration
- Time-span consideration
- Resources consideration

PROSPECT CONSIDERATION. Prospect means 'opportunities' or 'chances'. An entrepreneur, like Brenda Ratcliff, utilizes the 'prospect consideration' to decide the offers she accepts on her desk. As an experienced MC, presenter, trainer, and leadership coach, she knows when a client is coming on a trial basis or on an auxiliary mode (to use her services as a cover-up). In the former, she considers things like cost and availability of time in accepting a proposal. On the latter, there won't be a need to retain a customer who is not staying. Instead of filling her schedule with temporary clients, she decides it's best to save her time for more long-term ones instead. As an entrepreneur who has highly defined goals and plans for their business, you will need to know how to decipher one opportunity from another. That way, you stay on track to reach your goals.

PROFIT CONSIDERATION. This decision shares similar features with 'prospect.' While prospect consideration considers the sustenance of an offer, profit consideration focuses on the payout. If I can't get my targeted cost from a service or job, why take it on when there are better offers on the line? Businesses encounter losses in certain conditions, but this should not be why you take below-cost jobs. The profit attached to requests helps you decide what to accept. There is a kind of solid feeling that comes with well-paid jobs. You can also use this yardstick to tick off redundant schedules on your list. Things that don't make you money should be removed from the list.

TIME-SPAN CONSIDERATION. Some jobs end up taking up too much time in your day. If the task takes away the time you had allocated towards other projects, it should concern you. Some entrepreneurs use this to choose what offers to accept and which ones to turn down. Grant Johnson, a co-founder at Rocket spark, can tell you how much time it takes to create websites. If the offer is taking time away from the other jobs you have to do, and you're losing money. At this point, you should decide to stop the new project or be more careful when determining what extra work to take on.

COMFORT CONSIDERATION. Brenda Radcliff said, 'If I don't feel comfortable at the beginning of a project, there is no way I will feel comfortable later.' She makes her decisions based on 'its comfortability.' Doing discomforting tasks can be stressful. Nothing drains energy like that experience. You find it hard to concentrate, every little distraction gets to you, and you may end up not giving your best to it. So, why bother in the first place?

RESOURCES CONSIDERATION. This decision should not only be for production companies but for companies who depend on renewable resources. Every entrepreneur depends on materials, capital, and human resources for their businesses to thrive. They need to consider if the level of resources can handle the customer's offer. If the resources just aren't there, this is a yardstick to use and a way to determine what y choose to accept. When saying 'yes' when you don't have the available resources, consider the extra costs involved. Save yourself the stress from the beginning and copy the style of these successful entrepreneurs. Check the availability of your resources before deciding what to take on.

So far, we've discussed when to say 'YES.' Now, let's go over the times you should say 'NO.'

WHEN TO SAY NO (THE TRUE NO)

Saying 'yes' is ideal, but there are several times when you need to enforce your 'NO.' This should happen when:

- No preparation has been made
- It does not align with your priorities or goals
- You've reached your limit
- The goal is unrealistic

NO PREPARATION HAS BEEN MADE. In situations when you lack employees, back-ups, resources, and just about everything else needed to complete the job, you don't need a soothsayer to remind you that the correct answer should be "NO." While trying to measure up and cover limitations, don't make the mistake of accepting jobs that you're just not ready to take on.

IT DOES NOT ALIGN WITH YOUR PRIORITIES OR GOALS. Everyone has a goal. Serious entrepreneurs prioritize, and they have things they look up to when they do this. It helps them to achieve specific goals they have in mind. It's not beneficial for you to accept jobs that don't align with your goals and priorities. I use 'priorities' because sometimes, a career that is important to your goal might be imposing. However, it still needs consideration because the purpose is involved.

YOU'VE REACHED YOUR LIMIT: Testing your limits is good. But if accepting an offer is not growing your capabilities, it would be best not to take it on. It will reduce your productivity level, and that does not help.

THE GOAL IS UNREALISTIC. How does one recognize an unrealistic offer or task? As an entrepreneur, you should know what matches and what does not. If the service or product you offer will not be meaningful or yield good results, there are two things you should do. First, be sincere to the client and let them know. Second, say 'NO' to prove your point.

In conclusion, I'll use this example to demonstrate how I deal with situations like these. A customer asks me, 'can you do this job before the end of today?' I know we are already at 95% capacity, so I ask myself if I can do it. The answer I get is 'Yes, I can do it, but No, I don't want to do it.' I know this client will have many requirements and changes, so it will take longer than usual. However, he is a repeat customer, and I have known him for a long time. Then I consider how to professionally turn down his offer while keeping our business relationship intact. I'll ask myself, 'Should I make up some excuse like, we don't have enough materials? Or say there's not enough time because it will require an extra day of processing?' In the end, I tell him that we are at max production capacity.

Usually, if we are not busy, I will accept the job, and I don't have to charge a premium. However, in these scenarios, two things are needed to save the situation. One, tell the client, 'there will be no change of requirement. Once we finish, it's done. We don't have time to make any other changes or adjustments.' Two, I have to charge you extra to compensate for the overtime and additional labour costs. I will leave him the options to decide if he wants to proceed. Of course, if he decides not to move forward, it won't be a problem. But, I have to make sure the premium charge is an amount that is justified for me to go through this process.

Chapter 8
Taking A Break

"Taking a break means two things. First, selecting work that doesn't require brainpower and second, actually relaxing."

All business owners need rest. The reigning cliché 'all work and no play will make jack a dullard' makes a lot of sense when you think about it in this situation. Even designed robots rest to tell you that everything, both natural and cultural creations, deserve some rest to function better. I realize when I turn off my computer for a while, it functions better than when it's being used nonstop. It's also essential that an entrepreneur takes less brain-straining jobs for their sanity and efficiency. If you need to get the best result from everything you do, you should consider balancing things out. It's good to work, but it's also good to take care of your brain so that the system that provides you with energy and ideas will not break down.

There are workaholics whose mindset has been built to think a bit of rest is a waste of time. They work all the time. Stealing their resting time, eating time, and other good times, which readily should be used on their overall physical and mental well-being. It's because of this error that we provided a chapter on 'taking a break.' You don't have to feel guilty when you take a break or feel like you're wasting time when you take on less stressful work. You will achieve more if you take it easy on the heavy brain-draining tasks. The goal is not to break down. We all want to achieve more productivity in our work fields, and taking in too much would break us down. That's not part of the plan.

Are there reasons why someone who wants to achieve success would take fewer brain-straining jobs? The answer is definitely 'YES.' Some of these reasons are outlined and explained below.

REASONS YOU NEED TO TAKE A BREAK

If there are no reasons to take a break, no one would suggest it. But since there are, you need these ideas to guide your working efficiency. The reasons we will look at are:

- To keep you from getting bored
- To maintain focus and to think better
- To readjust your plans

TO KEEP YOU FROM GETTING BORED. Getting bored is one of the problematic situations a worker may face in his pursuit of success. I say this from experience. Suppose I'm working on a job and find nothing that interests me in the job anymore or find there's nothing adventurous or new to learn. In that case, I get worked up and don't want to finish the job. In the end, if I don't take the proper measures to get the zeal back, I produce terrible results. At this point, the only remedy is 'taking a break.' I find something that lifts my spirit and allows me to be distracted for a while. Sometimes, I take a walk, go for a swim, or do something entirely different from the brain-straining job. When I get back to it, I realize that some strength has been refilled. This is why taking a break is highly recommended. Most patients get a 'bed rest' prescription at hospitals as part of the plan to get their health back to normal. If you don't find a reason to rest, let the tedious nature and its damaging effect on your mental health force one on you.

TO MAINTAIN FOCUS AND THINK BETTER. A healthy mind thinks faster and processes better. Have you ever tried waking up in the early hours of the morning? The free feelings the mind gets at the moment are what taking a break does to the human mind. You will find that it's easier to come up with ideas. You will realize that if there is a task at hand during such moments, you will carry them out better than during a busy day with lots of activities. During the day, the only way to salvage the situation is by taking "a break." You don't have to feel guilty or that you have wasted your time for no good reason. When I was a little child, my father would always make a timetable and include a resting time for everyone called 'siesta.' I would find excuses to continue playing or studying or doing anything besides resting. One day, I fell ill and was taken to a clinic. The doctor said, "let him get enough rest." This example may not have aligned with the point, but taking breaks gives you better chances to focus on tasks and complete them. Instead of getting "all worked up" and finishing dead, take a break and refresh. Statistics say that many adults die on time because of stress. You can avoid this if you learn to take some time out from your daily schedule and just do nothing but rest.

Psychologically speaking, taking breaks heals your mind and gives your brain the time to process. An Uber Fact says that stress can reduce brain function up to 13%. I can attest to the truth of that. Whenever I'm stressed out, my brain is worked up, and I can't think straight. I don't trust myself to make significant decisions.

You tend to get pissed off easily when you are stressed out. You may yell at people over insignificant things. The importance of taking time out of your day to rest cannot be ignored. In this day and age, there's so much going on during the day. You have deadlines to meet, get stuck in traffic, need to get to the office before 8 am, need to submit a file, and need to sort out some emails or phone calls. In all this bustling and hustling, learn to take time out and rest. It will save your life.

TO READJUST YOUR PLANS. A CEO asked his secretary, who kept intruding in his work, to cancel one of the best offers he worked on getting. After he took a break and returned to his seat to get back to work, the secretary presented the file to him that he had asked her to cancel. To her surprise, he told her to approve it. The secretary questioned his request to cancel it earlier that day. The boss could only say, "I was not thinking straight."

This is the same thing you experience when you refuse to take breaks when they are necessary. You tend to make the wrong decisions. Your mind is filled with too many things, and you might not make the right decisions. This usually happens when there is a lot to do or when you are working on a deadline. You need a break because you have to come up with good results. A client will never accept 'I didn't get enough rest, that's why the quality is like this,' or 'there was no time to correct that mistake.' No good testimony will follow a poorly produced product or service. Therefore, the best option is to get as much rest as possible. If you feel taking an "actual rest" may not work, accepting less brain-straining jobs will.

Learn to cancel some schedules and plans. Call your colleague and inform him that you can't make it to the meeting (if the meeting is not a hundred dollars important).
Have some "Me" time, where all you do is sit down and stare, or lie down and rest. Put the phone down, or better still put it in flight mode. Shut down all other activities and reconnect with yourself.

ACTUAL RELAXATION
This chapter has gone over 'pausing' in between tasks to rest the brain a little. We've also emphasized the importance of taking less brain-straining jobs. Still, the idea of taking off a whole month from work has been neglected in this study. Does it mean it's not essential? Far from it. Taking breaks will help balance your productivity. It will also do your brain good if you maintain this focus for a few weeks or even an entire month. Of course, any serious entrepreneur understands the value of time. No one expects you to leave a client halfway through completing their job. When faced with such a situation, you can consider delegating functions to take your breaks.

I know of a public icon and entrepreneur, Edirin Edewor. She publishes posts, class updates, offline and online engagements, amongst other strenuous tasks. There was a time I didn't want to believe she was capable of doing all this until one of her posts confirmed she was taking some time off. She was away from all activities for about two weeks, but her office did not close down. She assigned managers to help her continue her work while she got her mental health restored. When she got back, it was obvious because she returned with a lot to offer. She even hinted at the importance of taking care of your physical well-being to better your mental health. That was all I needed. I will still reiterate how important it is to relax your mind when it's required. Learn just to go off sometimes. In the religious or even military world, you have what is called a "retreat." It's a period where they decide to withdraw from activities and rejuvenate. What ends up happening is they come back stronger and more ready to conquer their tasks. I think it's an excellent concept to adopt in your personal life too.

PHYSICAL "BREAK-TAKING" METHODS TO ADOPT
Physical attributes are what we make them. Research has come up with methods of achieving 'breaks' that set our minds at ease. Many entrepreneurs have tried these methods. Let's quickly look at two ways to take breaks and achieve physical break-taking ways you need to achieve valuable results. These methods are:

Bit-Bit Method and
Use of Apps

BIT-BIT METHOD. The name Bit-Bit implies that you complete your tasks gradually. Some writers also call it the "Pomodoro method," but I feel bit-bit's better. This method requires that you include breaks in your schedule. Let's say 'Twenty-five minutes.' If you have twenty-five tasks to do in a day, take a twenty-five-minute rest between every five tasks you complete. You can take a walk, put your head down and rest your brain or anything else that helps you as long as you take a break. When taking fewer brain-straining jobs, you may increase the number of tasks from ten to fifteen to twenty or twenty-five but still, make sure that you're leaving room for breaks.

USE OF APPS. Earlier in this book, I recommended using 'apps' to split work and ensure you completed all your scheduled work. The use of apps in this section is to help you regulate your activities and know when to take your breaks. Some don't remember their rest periods. They're not totally to blame. The best method to help you remember are apps like 'Desktime' and Draugien groups, amongst others. These apps notify you like an alarm. Even if you are engrossed in working and decide to put it on 'snooze,' it does not go off until you take your time to write 'rest' on the notepad in the app. The beauty of these apps is in their ability to help discipline your brain. It takes some determination to leave your work for a moment, especially when the job is to get a considerable amount of funds for that work. But this should not bother you. You need your rest to make even more money. This alone should convince you to do the right thing for yourself.

I set notifications in my smartphone to track my rest periods. When it signals me to rest, I rest. It's for my own good.

ACTIVITIES TO HELP YOUR MIND RELAX

When you are on these breaks or resting periods, there are recommended activities to help the mind relax. I know some people find it hard to force a break on themselves. It's to these people that I recommend the following healthy activities, which I also utilize to help my mind.

- Friend signalling
- Listening to music
- Going for lunch
- Playing games

FRIEND SIGNALING. A friend can also be a "co-worker" or a partner in this context. Friends can help you determine when you need a break. In large operating firms and even small ones, colleagues call their buddies during break times. Showing up for your friends and letting them show up for you at this point is advisable. This is why you need to have trusted backups. Be keen on choosing them. Make good friends who will keep you accountable at work. Jordan comes to hit my desk each time he's ready to leave for his recess. Sometimes, I want to ignore him or push him away, but he'll start a conversation and crack jokes until I give in and leave my desk for a while. I also ask my secretary to tell me when it gets to a specific time. I know I find it hard to keep to this routine, so I find people to help me. The idea is to get someone that will remind you to rest. Your co-worker can be that person. Your secretary can be that person. Your real-life friend or family member. It just has to be someone that will keep you accountable.

LISTENING TO MUSIC. Music is the first thing I would recommend to a workaholic. Music genres are made every season. Ambient music is proven to help calm the listener.

Some examples of this would be nature sounds, orchestra music, and down-tempo beats. Nature sounds include sounds of a waterfall, birds chirping, or rain. These types of sounds have been proven to revitalize one's mood and improve productivity. Orchestra music is said to help information retention. Anyone with insomnia or interval amnesia can use ambient music to help retain information or keep the brain active. Down-tempo is a genre called 'electronic dance.' It consists of hard beats that are meant to encourage dancing. It helps to boost your mood, secrete tranquillity and help you relax. Another type of music you should consider for your relaxation is 'Lo-fi.' This is a micro-genre, enabling you to study better. You can also try video game music and dynamics. When you go back to finish your work or start a new task, you'll realize that you have a sharper mind and better focus.

Music is highly therapeutic. Playing Enya's songs or Yanni's on a busy day can help you relax. The symphony of the musical instruments has a way of inducing relaxation and makes the soul stand on tiptoe. It washes off the stress on the soul and gives it some peace.

GOING FOR LUNCH. This may not seem important to some people, but eating helps the body focus. Do you notice that when you consume more food, energy is refilled? During your breaks, enjoy an excellent meal to ensure that you replenish your strength and are ready to finish your work. This is not restricted only to entrepreneurs. Everyone needs food to survive and be strong. Even while studying, if you have no energy, it'll be harder to concentrate. Any endeavour you require success in needs a good state of mind and body to function effectively. You can achieve this by making healthy meals. It will go a long way in ensuring that you achieve your goals.

PLAYING GAMES: This is the last recommendation and the funniest. Imagine coming into a business room and seeing your boss playing video games instead of typing or preparing a contract for a client. I do this sometimes too. It helps me relax. Games are healthy activities that don't take a lot of energy from you but provides relaxation and zeal to your body and mind. You should give yourself these treats sometimes. You will realize that productivity boosts will come in ways that you didn't expect.

To end this chapter, I will leave you with a story of how I deal with taking breaks.

Taking breaks means working on something that I don't need to use my brain to do. I usually start with cost savings first. I have to drive around to pick up materials from local suppliers, at least every other day. I don't want to overstock, and usually, when you stock 1 product, the client wants the other. Also, there are thousands and thousands of available products for our clients to choose from our trade show industry. I will usually try to select and recommend products from my local supplier. For my top 20% best-selling items, I will directly purchase them in bulk from China or the US. When I do pickups, I usually arrange my lunch at the same time. When everyone is on lunch, that's the best time for me to drive around, to pick up from local suppliers. This saves me a great deal of time and is a break for me since I don't have to overthink. The route is pretty much set, just like a Tesla autopilot to destination. While I'm at the supplier, I can chat with them about how the market is doing, any new products coming in, or the latest move in the industry. The topics are endless, even when I visit them every other day.

The idea is that you should have a hobby. It can be car racing games that you enjoy the most, anything that makes you happy and keeps you revitalized.

When I'm in the office and need a break, I usually walk around the building and warehouse to spot-check different things. I will check if clients have picked up any long-sitting orders or if my staff needs help to bring paperwork to the warehouse. When I'm at the warehouse, I usually check what my team is doing. Anything that doesn't look right to me, like how the inventory is placed or how things are organized. I also ask, 'are they following a work process that allows them to finish the job quickly and easily without justifying quality?' The majority of my team members have been with the company for over five years, and they know my expectations. Sometimes they can do an even better job than I can. If any new product or process needs to be invented, they will automatically come to me and ask for advice.

Chapter 9
Organizing Your Work With No-Cost Online Organizational Tool

"For every minute spent organizing, an hour is earned."

Neglecting to organize our day-to-day activities would lead to chaos in our lives.

As the world evolves so, does business. The business world faces a lot of tasks and challenges. A business corporation needs software engineers to build software applications that solve the rising challenges in today's corporate world.

Software engineers are developing different organizational tools and software to help us perform our work more effectively.

Organizational tools are software and computer program applications that help you perform tasks effectively.

There are many free tools available on the internet for you. These are some of the tools you can use to organize your work effectively.

The CANVA Tool

Canva.com is a tool that helps you design, create and customize logos, flyers, and graphic slides. Canva enables you to save time when improving your design with thousands of customizable templates. You can create your layouts without a pre-designed template. A good sketch on paper will give you an outline of how your design would look on CANVA to bring your design vision to fruition.

Here's a step-by-step approach to creating a better design on CANVA

1. Outline Your Design Dimensions
Start your design by choosing the correct dimension for your graphics design from the homepage. Each graphic design you'll make has its appropriate measurements, even if it's a simple social media post or a more complex graphic design.

2. Use an appropriate colour and background
Your graphics design background, colour, and images are essential.
Colours emit different emotional responses, and some colour combinations can be awful for your final design.
Use the CANVA's colour combination tool in the toolbar and pick the most suitable colour for your work.

3. Iterate your designs
Designs include text, figures, signs, and symbols. There should be a balance between your blueprint and its elements so your work can be more visually appealing.

4. Use the appropriate fonts for your design
Fonts impact design. The kind of fonts you choose for your design speaks volumes.
A particular font might not fit all types of designs. Canva has over a thousand font combinations. You can select the font combinations tool from the text tab.

You can also create your own font combinations but be sure it suits the purpose of your design. Unclear fonts will affect the way your audience perceives the message you are presenting.

Google Drive

Google Drive is an essential organizational tool that helps you store files in cloud storage. The purpose of this tool is to remove limitations to the storage capacity of your hard drive.

The online drive allows you to save information like PDFs, images, videos all on the Google server. It's a necessary tool for businesses because every user's account has a free 15GB storage capacity. Access to more storage would require you to subscribe to the paid plan.

If you want to use the Google Drive app, you will need a Gmail account to access the drive. You can edit, organize and share documents or files directly with colleagues.

Employees can synchronize information across all Internet-enabled devices. Data can get messy on your drive when lots of people share the same storage space or if documents are disorganized.

You should organize your documents with the following steps.

Structure your folders. Start by putting each document into its appropriate category folder. You can also use sub-folders or colour codes to itemize each document.

List view your documents. Instead of grid-viewing your files, you should list view them so you can see more files at a glimpse. You can change the viewing settings from the icon at the top right corner of the application interface.

Star urgent files you want to pass across to other team members. Starred files would stand out while browsing through them. Clicking on the starred icon will list all documents that you have indicated as urgent.

Delete old or finished projects from your drive. Don't clutter your drive with useless files that consume viable space.

The Asana software

Project management software like Asana.com makes project management easier compared to days without organizational tools. Asana is an organizational tool for businesses. It solves most business tasks like supervising projects, information gathering, etc.

Asana allows team members working on a particular project to share a single workspace and have easy access to information. Asana software depicts tasks as unique digital cards. The digital cards contain specific information about the work to be done.

All project information is backed up to the cloud storage automatically. Cloud storage enables real-time access to the project's data.

Here's how you should use Asana for your work

Start by setting up your projects. Choose your appropriate viewing style that suits the project's needs. There are several viewing styles you can choose from. They are list view, board view, calendar view, and timeline view. Pick your view style and select the correct template that makes your project accessible with little to no effort.

Create and assign your tasks. Create tasks on Asana using the "add task" button. You can document information, status, or deadlines to each assignment and designate assignments to team members directly from your workspace.

You should organize your tasks. Don't create a list of projects on Asana without a proper plan. Put your projects into urgency order, and design your work to suit the workflow or protocols

The Google Calendar App

Google calendar is essential for businesses that schedule employees.

This app can help businesses coordinate their schedules and create meetings.

You can create events on the calendar by adding your colleague's email addresses to the attendees and send out the invites to their emails.

Open the Google Calendar on the left-hand side, input your teammate's email under the calendar.

You need to request permission to view their calendar. Once it's accepted, you will be able to view your team member's calendars.

Scheduling meetings in your calendar is a lifesaver. Did you know you can easily create a Google Hangouts link so you can have virtual meetings? By adding a Google Hangouts link, the person invited to your meeting can easily find your event link in their calendar. This saves your time. You don't need to send a video conferencing link separately every time.

How you can create Hangout invite links from your calendar

Sign in to your Calendar App, create an Event, click More Options, select Hangouts, complete the rest of your event details, then Save.

Add a Hangout link to your Google Calendar.

Change Your Google Calendar view to Days, Weeks, Month,

or Year.

If your calendar is filled with events, changing the view can help give you a better idea of what's coming up. If you have an active type, a day view might be helpful so you can focus on all your meetings for that particular day. However, if you find you only have an event now and then, a monthly view might be better. You can change your perspective by:

Logging into the Google Calendar App, beside the Settings menu, click on the dropdown (Day, Week, Month, etc.)

Choose the setting you like to view your calendar in.

You can also choose to show weekends or not.

How to set event auto-reminders in Google Calendar App
Sign in to the Calendar App, click the Setting menu icon, and then scroll down to Settings for my calendars and click on your calendar

Scroll down to Event Notifications

Choose how much notice you need before events: minutes, hours, days, and weeks.

Choose whether to receive a notification or an email

Click on Add Notifications and Save.

The Dropbox and Dropbox Paper Tool

Dropbox.com is an organizing tool that lets you backup files to cloud storage and synchronize them to all your devices. When you sign up on Dropbox, you are allocated a 2GB storage capacity in an online storage facility. Dropbox has a new tool which is called Dropbox Paper. This tool allows you to create and share documents and arrange your documents in folders.

Dropbox paper is compatible with all media formats. This feature makes it the ideal tool for creating documents.

Here are some tips for using Dropbox Paper

1. YOU SHOULD CREATE INVITE-ONLY FOLDERS
Creating a folder in Dropbox Paper allows all the team members to view it. If you want only specific people on the team to view the folder, the best solution is to create an Invite-Only folder.
To create an Invite-Only folder, click on the Create A New folder button on the right panel. Once the new window appears, add the name. Next, click on the icon on the lower ribbon, and select Invite-Only.
Select the names of your team members, and hit the Create button.

2. USE THE POWER SEARCH BUTTON
Do you need to search for a document containing a specific word? The power search makes it possible. You will type the keyword on the search bar, and the relevant file or folder will come up immediately.
Similarly, you can search the documents through the title, and the tool will take care of the rest.

3. USE THE SHORTCUTS
In this jet age, everything is seemingly moving at the speed of light. You must follow the same mantra while managing your team on Dropbox Paper.

Dropbox Paper comes with an assortment of keyboard shortcuts. Apart from the general shortcuts like Ctrl+B for Bold and Ctrl+U for Underline, this collaboration tool supports a bevy of alternates. Some of them include:

Numbered List: 1. followed by a space.

Tasklist: [] followed by a space.

Header: Ctrl+Alt+1.

Date: /date followed by space.

If you have to add a series of tasks, add asterisks followed by space, and highlight instantly. With these, you save a lot of time going back and forth between the toolbar in a document. They also make your workflow more seamless.

4. CREATE TO-DO LISTS WITH EASE

To add a checklist of items, you need to input [] followed by a space. The good news is that you can assign these checklists/tasks on the go by simply adding an @ sign followed by the team member's name.

5. UPLOAD SCREENSHOTS EFFORTLESSLY

Dropbox Paper lets you upload screenshots and images easily. Here, you just copy the image from the source and paste it into your documents.

Also, rearranging images on Dropbox Paper is as easy as a drag and drop. Toggle your mouse pointer to the position and select the image you want to arrange.

THE WORDPRESS APPLICATION

WordPress is a web-publishing application that creates web pages without any web programming or design knowledge. It's an application where people can create their webpages, websites and blogs, requiring just a domain and hosting service. WordPress is where you will find millions of bloggers all over the world with their own peculiar and personal sites.

How to create a blog on WordPress

First, you need to have the WordPress application installed on your device or visit the site using any popular browser.

If you don't have a WordPress account, sign up for a new account. This requires a valid email that hasn't already been used on WordPress. Then, register with a username. Make sure it's unique.

After picking a username, choose a strong password. Your account is now created.

On the next page, you'll be required to fill in the name of your blog. You'll also fill in a description and primary goal for your site.

Next, choose an address for your blog. There's a free WordPress address option; however, you can decide to purchase one for an additional cost if you want a particular address.

Once you decide whether to use a free WordPress address or purchase one, your blog is officially created, and anyone can visit it.

THE WPS OFFICE

The Word Presentation Spreadsheet, popularly known as WPS office, is a software application that anyone can use anywhere in the world. It comes with lots of free features and can be used on any device. It has premium features that you can pay for, but the free features are also beneficial.

Features of WPS Office

You can save many files, documents, and spreadsheets on the WPS cloud. All you need to open a WPS cloud account is your email and a unique password.

You can create documents, spreadsheets, memos, PDFs and even scan photos or other forms.

Images can also be attached to documents.

Deleted files can always be recovered from the recycle bin. So, if you unintentionally deleted a file, you can always retrieve them. The recycle bin stores the deleted files for a set number of days before permanently deleting them.

When creating or editing files, you can choose several fonts, colours, or outlines.

DANGERS OF ONLINE ORGANIZATION TOOLS

We've looked at the various online organization tools, their features and their benefits. However, it's pertinent to note that there are also downsides to these tools. Therefore, be extremely careful not to suffer some damages or loss.

Data Exposure – Online file and data sharing tools are vulnerable to cyber-attacks, which involve hacking vital information.

Lack of security on devices - Sometimes, using our devices creates lots of security files, data, and processed data. When we use the devices the organization uses, there's a higher chance of protecting vital documents and information.

Negligence on the user - Users tend to share sensitive data and exchange information that could cause a breach of privacy. Sometimes, they forget to encrypt data.

Viruses - There are some search engines with viruses. Downloading corrupt applications and storing files on them can lead to loss of data and other vital documents.

HOW TO AVOID DANGERS ATTACHED WITH ONLINE ORGANIZATIONAL TOOLS

Ensure you set up an adequate security system. Data, information, files and other vital properties should be well secured. You can encrypt them or set codes and passwords that can't easily be hacked. Today, most organizations that have experienced losses take extreme measures to protect their information. As an organization, and you, as an individual, would not want to lose everything you've worked hard for. That's why taking measures to protect your documents and file is essential.

Avoid sharing personal details. We exchange lots of files, documents and data. One should be extremely careful not to send the wrong information. Take serious caution and, if possible, scrutinize the particular data you're sending or receiving.

For companies, competent people should be employed in handling data. An incompetent person is likely to make the company suffer a significant loss. To avoid such an experience, companies should be intentional about who they employ to run such delicate tasks.

Always be on the lookout for suspicious operations on your site. You can create settings that notify you if someone is trying to log in or hack into your site without your knowledge. That way, you can put extra measures in place to ensure your site is well secured. Once, I noticed that the password to my LinkedIn account was being tampered with. I tried a couple of times to log in. Instead, I was asked to change my password. I used a new password, but I still kept getting the same warning to change it. After repeatedly having this issue, I decided to use a highly complex code as my password so that way no one can hack into my account. Since then, my account hasn't experienced any sort of hitch.

Having listed all of these dangers and the measures to prevent them, it's up to you to take extra steps in protecting your properties online. As much as these online tools save us time and have their advantages, your data can become vulnerable. Take the steps we just discussed to make sure it doesn't happen to you. Thankfully, lots of people are sharing their experiences to create awareness. Checking them out would do a lot of help and save you from some painful loss of vital information.

The PayPal Tool

PayPal is an online payment tool suitable for small and big businesses. The Covid-19 pandemic made companies launch their businesses online (E-commerce). Every day thousands of products and services are bought and sold over the internet. PayPal acts as a bridge between sellers and buyers. PayPal facilitates secure payment channels between both parties. Using PayPal as your gateway for online payments would positively impact your business because PayPal comes with lots of benefits for both parties.

Businesses can pay employees through PayPal. You can create payroll for approximately 200 employees. Opening a business account allows you access to several features exclusively for businesses.

To set up a PayPal business account, you're required to submit pieces of information about your business. This includes email address, bank accounts details, and customer care hotline. Paypal verifies your information before allowing your account to receive and make payments without hassles.

Benefits of using PayPal as an online financial tool for your business

PayPal helps businesses process debit card payments and issue receipts to online customers. PayPal charges a business account 2.9% for each transaction. Charge rates change according to the terms and conditions.

PayPal provides credit opportunities for your customers. There are terms and conditions for this customer's loans.

PayPal also offers businesses the opportunity to take loans.

Paypal facilitates two types of loans for business accounts, business loans and working capital loans. You can apply for any of these loans if your business meets the criteria.

The business loan is for businesses that have been in existence for a minimum of 10 months and have an approximate yearly revenue of $42,000. A company that meets this criterion is eligible to apply for a loan ranging from $5000 to $500,000.

For you to access the working capital loan, your PayPal business account must meet the following requirements:

Your PayPal business account is over 100 days old.

Your account has transacted $15,000 within the past 12 months.

If your account meets these requirements, you're eligible for a working capital loan, ranging between $1,000 to $125,000. There's a stipulated amount of time for you to pay back the loan.

Organizing and optimizing your work is difficult without technology. The progression of technology has made it possible to organize your work with just a few clicks of a mouse. Most employees find it challenging to manage their work hours because of numerous projects they have to work on every day. Software engineers have developed software programs and computer applications that make you far more productive. Software programs can help you automate, optimize, and enhance with better collaboration from teammates.

These tools are essential for every business owner because it helps you create documents, presentations, and databases.

Here are a few benefits of using online organizational tools

1. Effective collaboration among team members
Online tools have made collaboration between team members easy. It has helped individuals focus on their respective tasks and share timely updates about their assignments or projects. These software applications allow you to get updates and notifications on projects and tasks. You can also host meetings, hangouts, and presentations via the same tool.

2. Confidentiality of information
Modern organizational tools have privacy policies. The security features never allow information shared between members in the system to be accessed by a non-member. All the information transmitted within the software is secure and stored in the internal system. These software tools comply with the standard guidelines for database security and privacy.

3. Better work experience for users

Visual features of organizational tools help you see and access information in a better way. Prioritize urgent documents so you don't forget them. The software makes it easier for you to know which documents your teammates have completed or are currently working on. Real-time feedback on the team's projects is easily accessible.

Only authorized persons and team leaders can make decisions, comments, and deadlines on tasks. This feature improves the system's efficiency. Handling a large number of team members is taxing. You might forget necessary files or less urgent projects. Online tools alert or notify you of project deadlines, and your team works progress. This feature helps members of any team meet deadlines and deliver optimal work.

4. Easy documentation of your work

Where your team members are located isn't a barrier with online tools. Access to information and documents isn't limited to a specific location. Team member's location makes it difficult to gather hard copy information and documents. With the online organizational tools, access to the project's data is done in minutes.

5. Job satisfaction

Your productivity on a project is directly related to how satisfying it is. If you're inspired, you will produce more efficient work. Using online tools can ease your workload and motivate you and your team to deliver far more effective work. You'll receive a greater sense of satisfaction from the ease of completing your everyday tasks.

CONCLUSION

This book should propel you to perform your work expertly. You can do more in no time if you follow the simple guidelines in the book.

As a business owner or entrepreneur, honesty should be your mantra. Being honest to customers, colleagues or teammates improves these relationships. When you start a project, you should state your goals clearly, and share them with the public. Goals that aren't broken down into sections are usually challenging to achieve. You should break down your goal into phases and celebrate each milestone you reach.

Perfection is an illusion, and there's no such thing as perfect. As humans, we don't get perfect; we get better. Don't allow the fear of being imperfect to stop you from achieving your goals. Making your work perfect can be demanding because there's always room for improvement. Your job is okay as long as it delivers the desired results. Perfectionism sometimes can be a personal problem that we transfer to our business. If you're a perfectionist with your day-to-day activities, you will transfer it to your work. Trying to produce excellent work might lead to a loss of interest in the job.

Always have a plan for your day. Starting your day without a plan makes the day rule you. To achieve your goals, you should write them down each night for the next day. You should start with the most critical task and move on to the less important ones. Following this routine daily will give you the momentum to conquer your daily goals. Making plans is one of the best things anyone can do to become more productive. It holds various opportunities that cannot be accessed if not tried.

While you take planning and multitasking into consideration, remember to take a rest. In today's world, many things compete for our attention, and you need to set your priorities to make the most of your day. Take a twenty-minute break for every two uninterrupted hours of work. These breaks help reduce fatigue and increase concentration.

Time management is an essential discipline every entrepreneur should have. You can make more money but not more time. We all have 24 hours per day. You can never get enough time, but you must maximize your effort to utilize your time and complete your daily tasks.

To effectively manage your time, break your work into smaller chunks and allocate a specific amount of time to each task. Several online applications help you manage your time and stay focused. You can't avoid distractions at work. There's always distraction around us, but you have to work around them. Use the distraction as stepping stones, block off the bad distraction and allow good distractions instead. Keep away from your phone or use the do-not-disturb feature so you don't get distracted by calls or notifications while working.

Develop a multitasking mindset. It will help you get more things done in less time. Multitasking is not about handling multiple projects at once. It's the ability to focus on a particular task and get it done efficiently. Your work environment might not show you the liberty of focusing on a specific project at a time. However, attending to different tasks and still getting the job done comes from a multitasking mindset.

You will get overwhelmed if you say 'Yes' to every task that comes to your table. Learn how to say no to jobs that you can't handle. Saying no is very difficult for most people. Our society has taught us to say 'Yes' and feel guilty when saying 'No.' Most times, our gut tells us to say 'No,' but we go against it. You should follow your instincts whenever you want to make decisions. I know you want to say 'Yes' because opportunities only come once. The best opportunity would be lucrative and appealing to you. If you say 'Yes' to every opportunity that comes your way, you'll spread yourself too thin. When you overwhelm yourself with work, you'll be frustrated and unproductive. Learn how to refuse an opportunity that doesn't go well with you. Only focus on a single project at once. You are pursuing success, but the most successful people on earth didn't say 'Yes' to every opportunity that came knocking at their door. You'll be amazed by the number of opportunities they declined to be successful.

Aside from planning, multitasking, taking breaks, managing your time, getting the notion of imperfection and perfection as a worker, knowing what to accept in your business lane and what not to accept, you must understand that every entrepreneur is required to have a resilient spirit. The essence of this is that there are many problems that you will encounter on your way to becoming successful. This is not just about improving your productivity level. It's also about doing things more efficiently. You are expected by everyone, customers, and relations alike to learn and build resilience. It is a significant feature that will keep you going.

This book has extended its tentacles and given you examples that will help you become better. There are more relatable stories that should convince you as a reader to follow what works. Are there more reasons you need to implement these strategies in your business? There are many. I'm sure there are plenty of other examples if you cannot relate to the ones I have given you. But, to what do we owe all these? We desire implementation and betterment. Our watchword has always been 'to improve and become.'

Just For You

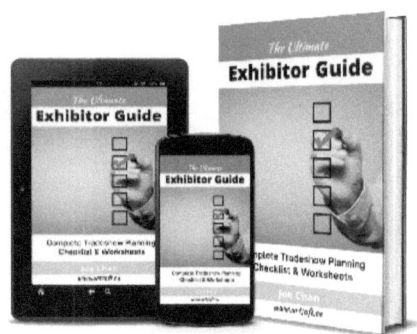

Hi, I'm Joe Chan and thanks for grabbing a copy of my "Work Smarter, Not Harder" self-help book. If you planning to exhibit in a tradeshow, this will be perfect guide for you, "The Ultimate Exhibitor Guide: Tradeshow Planning Checklist and Worksheet"! It's absolutely FREE! Before we get to it, I'd like to give a quick introduction about myself – who I am and what you can expect from this guide.

In a nutshell, I have been in the tradeshow industry for over 15 years. My company's name is called Artsoft Expo Solutions Inc. (www.artsoft.ca). We provide complete tradeshow display solutions – from off-the-shelf portable display to fully customized structure system. You can visit our Facebook page at www.facebook.com/artsoftexpo for some of the displays we have built in the last 15 years. Due to the pandemic, my business has been at a halt. However, it actually gives me time to sit down and rethink what I would like to do in my next 15 years. I came across an idea of self-publishing and I would love to share my personal tradeshow experience and hopefully will inspire some of you.

Everything I said in this guide came from my own personal experience of planning a tradeshow or exhibition. With this planning checklist and worksheet, I hope I can help save you some invaluable time and that you can acquire more ROI from your next tradeshow.

Let's get into the Ultimate Tradeshow Planning Checklist and Worksheet now! I hope you enjoy this guide.

SIGN UP NOW @ http://www.artsoft.ca/exhibitinglife/

References

20 Tips on How to Prioritize Work and Meet Deadlines. (2019, January 13). ThriveYard. https://www.thriveyard.com/20-tips-on-how-to-prioritize-work-and-meet-deadlines/

Alton, L. (2021, January 29). *5 ways productive business owners fight through distractions and stay focused.* The American Genius. https://theamericangenius.com/entrepreneur/5-ways-productive-business-owners-stay-focused/

Baker, L. (2021, February 17). *7 Ways Perfection is Killing Your Business – or Is It 6?* Small Business Trends. https://smallbiztrends.com/2016/09/business-problems-with-perfection.html

C. (2018, January 21). *How to Use Your Commute Time Wisely.* Creative Circle Digital + Creative Staffing. https://www.creativecircle.com/blog/use-commute-time-wisely/

Choi, J. (2020, June 19). *4 Ways You're Lying to Yourself About Being Productive.* The Muse. https://www.themuse.com/advice/4-ways-youre-lying-to-yourself-about-being-productive

Ellwood, M. (2018, September 17). *Time Crunch: An*

Entrepreneur's Guide to Prioritizing Your Tasks. Business.Com. https://www.business.com/articles/entrepreneur-prioritize-tasks/

Fahrer, C. (2018, October 3). *Optimization Mindset | Improve your company performance bottom-up.* OpsTales. https://opstales.com/creating-an-optimization-mindset/

How and Why We Lie at Work. (2015, January 5). Harvard Business Review. https://hbr.org/2015/01/how-and-why-we-lie-at-work

Hutchins, C. (2018, July 9). *5 Reasons Why You Should Always Say Yes, Even When the Answer is No.* Entrepreneur. https://www.entrepreneur.com/article/316018

Maynard, W. (2019, March 18). *Perfectionism is Your Worst Enemy as an Entrepreneur.* Wendy Maynard. https://wendymaynard.com/entrepreneur-is-perfectionism-holding-you-back-from-the-level-of-success-you-desire/

Pereira, D. (2018, June 29). *The Power of a Can-Do Attitude: Why Smart CEOs Always Say Yes.* StartupNation. https://startupnation.com/grow-your-business/attitude-smart-ceos-say-yes/

Photos, T. (2016, November 23). *8 ways to multi-task without getting stressed.* The Economic Times. https://economictimes.indiatimes.com/work-career/8-ways-to-multi-task-without-getting-stressed/break-the-reward-loop/slideshow/55579069.cms

Reiff, L. (2019, August 27). *The Reason You Shouldn't Lie to Yourself - The Understanding Project.* Medium. https://medium.com/the-understanding-project/the-reason-you-shouldnt-lie-to-yourself-79f03835659d

Ryan, L. (2016, May 18). *Five Lies About Self-Employment*

Most People Believe. Forbes. https://www.forbes.com/sites/lizryan/2016/05/18/five-lies-about-self-employment-most-people-believe/?sh=663893f62256

Schubert, A. (2021, March 30). *13 Things That Could Happen When You Quit Social Media*. The Healthy. https://www.thehealthy.com/mental-health/quit-social-media/

Seiter, C. (2020, June 30). *The Science of Breaks at Work: Change Your Thinking About Downtime*. Buffer Resources. https://buffer.com/resources/science-taking-breaks-at-work/

Shih, C. (2013, August 7). *Stop Lying to Yourself*. Lifehack. https://www.lifehack.org/articles/communication/stop-lying-yourself.html

Ward, E. (2020, January 21). *Soothing, minimal music scientifically linked to higher levels of concentration and productivity*. The Prospector. https://www.theprospectordaily.com/2020/01/21/soothing-minimal-music-scientifically-linked-to-higher-levels-of-concentration-and-productivity/

Young, S. H. (2019, April 8). *22 Tips for Effective Deadlines*. Lifehack. https://www.lifehack.org/articles/featured/22-tips-for-effective-deadlines.html

www.ingramcontent.com/pod-product-compliance
Lightning Source LLC
Chambersburg PA
CBHW031423210526
45464CB00005B/2027